C000143232

'Chris's first book, *Ordinary* [...]
be church "on the margins [...]
because it will help you to [...]
stories of struggle, self-do[...]
the midst of lack will resonate with many working in similar
situations. This book should be read by everyone finishing
their fifth year in similar situations. In other words, just
before you give up. It will keep you going with renewed
hope.'
Neil Hudson, author, Elim Pastor, formerly LICC

'In a church whose leaders can feel under pressure for
immediate, measurable success, this courageous book
reminds us that the mess that we human beings make of our
lives is the place where God goes to work. Chris Lane draws
on years of ministry in one of the toughest communities in
the country to set up a thrilling and insightful dialogue
between the narrative of the Scriptures and the challenges of
urban church life. The wise and practical conclusions he
draws will offer precious reassurance to urban church
leaders as well as inspire all with a call to ministry.'
Bishop Philip North, Bishop of Burnley

'Humorous, honest, heart-felt, hope-filled. Salford estate
church planter and pioneer theologian, Chris Lane, invites us
with courage and faith into dark deserts and wilderness
wastelands. Stories packed with wit and grit: I have laughed
and cried within pages. Again. And again. Holding up the
lamp of the Word, fired by the Spirit, Chris unearths the
underground treasures of Jesus' ordinary miracles, heaven
breaking into forgotten places. Once read, never forgotten.'
Bishop Jill Duff, Bishop of Lancaster

'In this book Chris Lane brings together two of his primary gifts. His love of teaching the whole biblical narrative – when many Christians only know their favourite passages – and his long experience of planting a church into an estate. His book provides both practical wisdom and biblical resources for anyone called to share in the patient mission of God in marginalised communities and, equally important, the lessons such churches have to teach the rest of us.'

Graham Cray, author, former leader of the Fresh Expression Team and chair of the Soul Survivor Trust

'This is an absolute gem of a book. Chris Lane writes with honesty and humour about his experience of planting in an urban estate in the North West. His passion for Jesus and for people is infectious. Weaving personal anecdotes through a stunning overview of the whole narrative of Scripture, Chris reminds us of the core truths that God uses unlikely people and seeks our faithful obedience rather than our success. If you are looking for a ten-step guide to church-planting then this isn't the book for you, but if you want a generous dose of the reality of urban ministry coupled with the miraculous "just enough" provision of God, then dive on in. This book made me cry, laugh and want to serve Jesus more. I heartily recommend it to you.'

Rev Dr Hannah Steele, London Monday Centre Director, St Mellitus College, author of Living His Story

'He's done it again.
'Of course, you might want a How To Lead a Successful, Triumphant, Pain-free Church That No One Will Leave and Everyone Will Join book. The trouble with such a book is that it will have been written by someone who has never read the Bible or been involved in church. And while you might want

to read that kind of book, you don't need to, because it won't do you any favours at all.

'But if you have been part of church for longer than five minutes you will recognise the hope and agony, the joy and sorrow, the vision and heartache that goes with belonging and investing in the community of Jesus Christ. But you won't simply recognise yourself in it, your eyes will also be opened to what can be all too easy to miss in the complexity of it – what God is doing through it all.

'Weaving together stories of vulnerability and hope with the story of God from Scripture, Chris shows himself to be what those of us who know him and esteem him value most about him – a profoundly hopeful and truthful teacher of the faith.

'This man is an utter gift to the church. Read this book now. Then immediately give it to someone else. This might possibly be the most important book for anyone involved in church planting to read.'

Rev Canon Chris Russell, Archbishop of Canterbury's Advisor for Evangelism and Witness

'The stories we tell shape the people we become. In *Not Forgotten*, Chris Lane, a masterful storyteller, gives us a kaleidoscope of hopeful and precious stories from the Bible and his own real-life experience of a difficult church situation. All together these stories are carefully honed to remind us all who we are in Christ -- fiercely and passionately loved, whatever our faults and frailties. In telling these stories with honesty and humour, and applying them to our everyday situations, Chris testifies to the good news that God is alive and kicking in the world and that the story of our adventure with Him isn't finished yet, however badly things might go and however tired or fed-up we might become.

'So, whoever you are, whatever your story, you are welcome here, you are not forgotten, because the God Chris loves loves you too: come and be refreshed and revitalised – it's like a spa for the soul! Read on, friends, and see how the Big Story of God emerges in every little story that Chris tells and notice afresh how God is at work in your story too, wanting to bring hope, transformation and healing by the Holy Spirit to help us write the next chapter of our stories with courage.'

Rev Canon Dr Michael Leyden, Dean of Emmanuel Theological College

'Chris and Esther have discovered the secret, that the kingdom of God is advancing at the beautiful blurry edges. The edges of our comfort zones, our capacity and our faith. The edges of our communities, our society, our expectations. Jesus is at work in the margins of life, not just on main stages. This book invites us all to see the God of all hope, in places, people and situations that are surely not forgotten, both in Scripture and in the story of our own lives. I am grateful for its message and the courage it stirs in me.'

Miriam Swanson, Fusion Movement

NOT FORGOTTEN

Chris Lane

instant
ap□stle

First published in Great Britain in 2022

Instant Apostle
104 The Drive
Rickmansworth
Herts
WD3 4DU

Every effort has been made to seek permission to use copyright material reproduced in this book. The publisher apologises for those cases where permission might not have been sought and, if notified, will formally seek permission at the earliest opportunity.

The views and opinions expressed in this work are those of the author and do not necessarily reflect the views and opinions of the publisher.

British Library Cataloguing-in-Publication Data

A catalogue record for this book is available from the British Library.

This book and all other Instant Apostle books are available from Instant Apostle:

Website: www.instantapostle.com

Email: info@instantapostle.com

ISBN 978-1-912726-58-5

Printed in Great Britain.

Acknowledgements

Esther: it's been quite a journey but we are still here! You bring the wisdom, consistency, prophetic insight and organisational skills as well as the electric blanket. You're the best.

Daniel: with your calmness, humour and shhh. Rebekah: with your energy, musical talent and RNLI knowledge. Hannah: making us all laugh, knowing about every bird and being a force of nature. I couldn't ask for three more brilliant children.

Andrew, Beth and Liz: it's hard to express the joy of leading church with three of my closest friends and favourite people. We have laughed and cried a lot these last few years and it's all been worthwhile.

Everyone at LCC: you are the most wonderful group of people and I love spending my life with you. Thanks for your commitment, love and perseverance (and general craziness).

To Mum and Dad, Gill and Rafael (and The Ten), Andrew and Natalie, Amelia and Emma, Ruth and Tom, Izzy, Will and Nancy, Joan and Nick, Gwen, Barbara and Patrick: thank you for all your support in so many ways.

To all who kindly agreed to read this for me, either to offer comments or endorsements, thank you so much: Hannah Wallace, Anina Thomas, Thomas Dean, Sam

Durdant-Hollamby, Esther Lane, Sarah Casson, Michael Leyden, Jill Duff, Philip North, Miriam Swanson, Graham Cray, Pete Greig, Hannah Steele, Chris Russell and Neil Hudson.

Thanks to all my brilliant colleagues and students at St Mellitus College and Emmanuel Theological College: I've learned so much from you all.

For all those who agreed to be interviewed and share some of your stories: Joe, Sophie, Hana, Ben, Amy, Robin, Judy, Sam DH, Katy, Thomas, Claudia, Sam W, Anna P. You are all such an inspiration to me.

Mike Pilavachi: thanks so much for writing the foreword, and much more so for all the support and kindness you have shown to me and LCC over so many years.

Massive thanks to Kenton for so generously supporting me to free up my time to write, and for all the prophetic wisdom you have given to me.

To all who have looked out for our little church over these tough few years: you have given us the courage to keep going and to hope and believe for better days ahead.

Contents

Foreword, Mike Pilavachi 17

Foreword, Pete Greig 21

Preface 25

Introduction.. 27

Chapter One: *Tohu* and *Bohu*....................................... 33

Chapter Two: Abram and Sarai.. 43

Chapter Three: Moses and Miriam 58

Chapter Four: Unlikely Leaders 72

Chapter Five: The Miracle of Just Enough 86

Chapter Six: Exile and Return... 101

Chapter Seven: Hearing the Gospel................................ 114

Chapter Eight: Not Forgotten 132

Chapter Nine: The Cross 153

Chapter Ten: Resurrection... 165

Conclusion 177

Contents

Foreword
Mike Pilavachi

Every now and then a book comes along that takes my breath away and significantly affects my understanding of the purposes of God in our times. When the book is written by a dear friend, as this one is, the joy and wonder at the revelations within is magnified. So before I talk about the book, a few words about the author.

I have known Chris Lane, his wife, Esther, and some of their mates for more than twenty-five years. Chris is one of the most humble, passionate, kind and normal human beings I know. His love for, and pursuit of, Jesus has been both a challenge and encouragement to me for many years. I have watched as he has consistently pursued God rather than glory, and sought a lifestyle of obedience instead of ambition for his own reputation, advancement and fame. I love and respect this man enormously. He is one of those whose example and encouragement have kept me going over the years. As well as being a brilliant theologian and communicator, a leader of Langworthy Community Church and an encourager of many other leaders who are serving in the margins and the tougher communities in our nation, he has served for years as a trustee of Soul Survivor, the movement that I had the privilege to serve for twenty-seven years.

And so to the book. I honestly believe that *Not Forgotten* is a prophetic and timely book for the age in which we live. Certainly anyone in a position of leadership in the Church should read this, but it is also essential for all those whose desire is to give themselves wholeheartedly to Jesus and His cause. Here Chris recounts the story of Langworthy Community Church in Salford with the ups and downs, the joys and sorrows and the laughter and the tears in a vulnerable, humble and accessible way.

This is a story of a group of friends who obeyed God's call to move into a troubled estate, to plant a church to be an expression of the kingdom of God in the midst of the pain, brokenness and anger that was all around. And then stayed. Stayed for years. To love and to serve and to pour themselves out. And they are still there. The story is at times heart-breaking but always heart-warming. Chris also shares stories of friends who are seeking to do the same things in many parts of the United Kingdom. At the same time, he interweaves the stories of Scripture in a way that brings both revelation and illumination. Indeed, the Bible teaching contained in this book is like a breath of fresh air after being stuck in a windowless room for far too long. Chris' fresh insights into familiar stories made me want to shout out in amazement and joy as well as the wonder of, 'Why didn't I see this before?!'

As I look at the story of the Bible and the history of the Church, I am more and more convinced that new moves of God begin on the margins and not in the centre. With the poor and not the rich. In the Bethlehems and not the Jerusalems. God chooses 'the foolish things of the world to shame the wise ... the weak things ... to shame the strong (1 Corinthians 1:27).

Over the last years, many of us in Christ's Church have bought in to a culture of both celebrity and consumerism, of image and branding. We have been mesmerised by success as defined by numbers and wealth and visibility. And it has not taken us very far. We mistook our busyness for fruitfulness. We have been busy rearranging the deckchairs while the *Titanic* sinks, aiming to draw large crowds while forgetting others are slipping out the back door, disillusioned and hurt. *Not Forgotten* is both a wake-up call and a practical demonstration of a better way, a more biblical way, a more humble way.

In a world where we parade our successes on social media, Chris calls us back to investing in obscurity. To feed the hungry without feeling compelled to issue a press release announcing what we've done. Indeed, to follow the example of our Lord. He was born in a stable and lived in obscurity on the wrong side of the tracks for thirty years. In his three years of ministry He never went further than 100 miles from his birthplace. Whenever He drew a crowd He either offended them so they left or He disappeared up a mountain or into the desert. Ultimately, He died the isolated, forsaken death of a common criminal on a lonely hill outside the city.

Chris encourages us to let go of consumer Christianity and points us to another way, a better story. A story of ordinary disciples who, together, wash the feet of their neighbours, love them consistently, have the patience and perseverance to serve them in season and out of season, and find themselves being transformed in the process.

This is a magnificent, honest, thoughtful, practical and encouraging book. I commend it to you.

Mike Pilavachi
Soul Survivor

Foreword
A river, a Bible and a broken heart, by Pete Greig

'There are three things a songwriter needs,' observes the Californian rocker Lee Bob Watson: 'A river, a bible and a broken heart.' The river, he says, gives you a sense of time and place. The Bible is the great archetypal keeper of meaning and language. And as for the broken heart – well, that's just a bitter-sweet occupational hazard for us all.

This, then, is a book about a river, a Bible and a broken heart.

First, it's about a river, by which I mean a particular place, an actual context bigger and even older than Chris himself. For him this is a patch of inner-city Salford called Langworthy, where he and his wife Esther planted a church in 2004, which continues to inform, inspire and infuriate them in equal measure. When Chris prays, 'Let your Kingdom come on earth as in heaven,' he means the schools and shops of Langworthy. And when Boney M sings Psalm 137: 'By the rivers of Babylon, there we sat down, yea, we wept when we remembered Zion' (NKJV), Chris is undoubtedly humming along thinking about the streets of Salford.

'So what's this got to do with me, then?' you may well ask, living as you do in Swindon, or Sutton, or Solihull? And the answer is, 'Everything!' We all have our own rivers. We find ourselves rooted in place and time, trying to work out what on earth the kingdom of God looks like here and now, outside TK Maxx on a rainy Saturday morning. Chris' context, and the contexts of the others whose stories he shares so generously, makes his message real and relevant for us all, free from the kind of disembodied hype that prevails in so many Christian contexts.

Second, this book is inspired by the Bible. Chris isn't just sitting around weeping by the river; he's actively listening to God for its people, applying the Word to the world in which he finds himself. And this is a big thing to say because Chris is a guy who really knows his stuff when it comes to the Bible. Amidst all the anecdotes and characters in this book, deep biblical truths are unpacked. It's the best kind of teaching – the sort that sneaks up on you disguised as a story and starts shaping you subtly without ever being boring.

But the best thing about this book is the fact that it's written with complete and compelling honesty by a man whose heart has clearly been broken. Chris is honest about the very real struggles and disappointments of ministry, especially in recent years. He doesn't feel the need to pretend. But he's also honest, uncynical about the enduring hope that 'compels us'. You can't change the church into anything new until you love her as she already is, and Chris clearly carries a deep and tender affection for her. I can almost hear all the sighs of relief around the country as people discover that they're really not alone.

I first met Chris more than twenty years ago, staying with him and Esther in their lovely two-up, two-down terraced home on an estate in Salford where many of the other houses had been boarded up. All these years later and they're still there, slogging away faithfully, sitting down by that same river, with a Bible giving voice to their lives, and the kinds of insights that only come from a truly, deeply broken heart.

Pete Greig
~ 24-7 Prayer International and Emmaus Rd churches

Preface

My first book, *Ordinary Miracles*, which was released in the summer of 2017, told the story of our life and work in the Langworthy estate in Salford, Greater Manchester, over the past couple of decades. In a place notorious for crime and deprivation, we encountered beauty, creativity, resilience and hope as we shared the gospel, our lives and our tables. *Ordinary Miracles* was my attempt to capture some of that learning and tell some of the stories of transformation and heartache that we experienced as we planted a new church: Langworthy Community Church.

Not Forgotten picks up the story in the aftermath of a tumultuous summer when our church was reeling from an incredibly difficult few months, praying and wondering what the future might look like. During that time, I started working part-time at St Mellitus College alongside my work with the church, helping to train pioneers and church planters across the UK, as well as starting a small network of churches to support people who are planting and leading churches in urban estate contexts. This has brought me into contact with lots of people who are doing exciting and creative work in all kinds of contexts around the country, often 'under the radar' but slowly and quietly seeing wonderful things happen.

In these pages you will read some reflections of our own experiences of being church in a very difficult time, and how God has met with us in the pain and struggle – in the wilderness. I also weave in other voices and stories – friends who find themselves called to live and work in places often referred to as 'forgotten estates' – and who have discovered that God has not forgotten them. All of this is in the framework of the Big Story of the Bible, which from the very first chapter teaches us about a God who speaks light into darkness, brings order from chaos and causes streams to flow in deserts. A God who chooses the most unlikely people to show the world what it is to be fully alive, how to love and to serve and to bring hope.

My prayer is that you will also find hope in these stories of the unlikely people and places, whether from the Bible or from the present day. I pray that you will gain a fresh love for Jesus, and for the Bible, and that God would give you courage and fresh vision. Remember that you are not forgotten. God sees you, and is full of compassion for you.

Chris Lane
January 2022

Introduction

'What the heck is happening?'

I was sitting in the garden of a conference centre in rural Derbyshire. On the other end of the phone line, my friend and fellow church leader, Beth, had just said a rude word. It wasn't actually the word 'heck'. I hadn't heard her say this word before, and I haven't heard her say it since. It's the kind of word that makes a film into a 15 certificate, or puts a Parental Advisory notice on an album. But it didn't seem out of place in this particular moment.

After we had finished talking, I was reeling from what I had heard and from the knowledge of what we now needed to do, and I quietly sneaked back into the St Mellitus College staff retreat. The staff were singing a song of worship and praying for each other. I sat there, stunned, staring blankly. A friend of mine, Hannah, walked over and asked if she could pray for me. I quietly said, 'Yes, but I might cry!'

I cried.

I felt so confused. Where was God in all this? How would we get through it? Would our little church survive? I had just returned from a glorious summer, preaching at various Christian festivals, telling the stories of our church and the transformation we had seen over the previous couple of decades. I had met inspiring people, received prophetic inspiration and had returned to Salford full of vision and hope for the next term. I was hopeful that this could be the start of the move of God we had been praying for all these years.

I arrived home from my summer of inspiration to an autumn of disasters. The details of what had happened are not appropriate to share, but owing to two or three major issues among our core team (which all came totally out of the blue), our small church lost almost half of our regular Sunday attenders within one month, and the pastoral fallout lasted for much longer than that. We were launched into many months of struggle, trying to look after a hurting church that was devastated by what had happened, while still trying to maintain our many outreaches into the local community. We were left with a huge hole in our already stretched resources, and were unable to run our public Sunday gatherings in the local school for a period of nine months.

During those nine months we were stretched to capacity trying to look after people who were struggling, hurting and confused. There were many sleepless nights, tears and some meetings that involved shouting (I don't like those meetings). On a number of occasions, I asked God if He was wanting us to close the church down, but all the words we heard back were of encouragement and perseverance. Songs about brokenness and God's church rising up again echoed around my confused little brain.

All through this time people would call me up and ask to visit the church, to learn from us! 'Hi, I heard you preach at a conference/read your book, I would love to bring a team to visit your church.' I would sit there thinking, 'There may not be a church for you to see!' It seemed strange that our story was inspiring people all over the place, while it felt like everything was falling apart at the seams – like trying to grasp sand in your hands, and it all overflows onto the floor. And this was all before a global pandemic sent the whole world into disarray.

In this book I want to share with you some of the things God has been teaching us in this dark time. It is particularly in these times that I think we have much to learn from small churches that are apparently struggling to survive in difficult places. I would like to tell some stories not just of our own experiences in Langworthy, but also of friends of mine whom God has called to plant churches in some of the forgotten estates of our country.

I honestly believe that some of the deepest learning and most important truths that the Church needs to hear are coming from the estates and marginalised communities – the 'forgotten' places and people. Just when the Church is announcing yet more gloomy figures of decline in attendance, there are utterly beautiful things happening on the margins. God is at work! In a time where politicians are talking about forgotten places and people – whether rural areas, urban estates or even whole regions – God is doing a new thing. These places and the wonderful people who live there are not forgotten by God. There is creativity and innovation, new life, streams flowing in the desert, lights shining brightly. I want to tell some of these stories of hope. I won't provide you with Six Simple Steps to Transform Your Community. There won't be many tweetable phrases or rags-to-riches tales. We won't be going From Good to Great, and we certainly won't go viral. But I hope you will be encouraged in your own walk with Jesus, and inspired to keep going, to keep loving, to keep sharing the glorious good news of Jesus in the places God has called you to be.

Growing up in a Brethren church gave me a love for the Bible. Auntie Joyce (not my actual auntie, but we called most of the adults in church uncle and auntie in those days) would set all the kids a challenge. If we could learn all sixty-six books of the Bible in the correct order, she would give us a box of sweets. I will never forget sitting next to my mum, speaking down the phone to Auntie Joyce, '1 John, 2 John, 3 John, Jude, *Revelation*!' And then we would have the grand presentation of the sweets on the Sunday.

One of my favourite games at church was where we had to hold our Bibles in the air, then someone would shout out a verse: 'John 3:16!' The first person to find it was the winner. I was very good at that game. We had competitions with prizes for memorising verses and even whole sections of Scripture, and loved singing songs by the well-known children's worship leader Ishmael, which were word-for-word Bible verses set to music.

That immersion in Scripture was just normal for me and some of my mates; it was the air we breathed. During a boring sermon we would sit at the back looking up the rudest bits in the Bible and giggling together (it was the days before mobile phones… OK, we were geeks!). The biblical characters, sayings and stories we learned as kids would live with us into adulthood, shaping our consciences, informing our decisions, giving us a lens through which to see the world.

When I started to lead some youth work at a church later on in life, I was shocked at the lack of biblical knowledge in the young people – they loved Jesus, they were great at hearing God speak and praying for each other, and passionate about reaching their friends, but they didn't know whether John the Baptist was in the Old or New Testament. There was a lot of fire there, but not enough fuel. As a kid in the Brethren, it was the other way round. Plenty of fuel, but we were wary of the fire!

When the fire of the Spirit lights the fuel of the Scriptures, that's when things get really exciting. I watched it happen as my childhood church experienced a charismatic renewal. It was amazing to see our youth group come alive and begin to experience – in our day – the reality of some of the stories we had learned in the Bible. It wasn't just a quick, impressive spark that quickly burned out but a fire that lasted and spread way beyond our little group.

Over the last few years, I have often reflected on how the Bible has shaped our story here in Langworthy – inspiring us, urging us on, giving us stories and pictures to explain our experiences. I have spoken to friends who are involved in similar pioneering ministries across the UK, and pressed them with questions about their own engagement with the Bible.

What I want to do in this book is to use the framework of the scriptural story to present some of the learning that is emerging from a quiet revolution that I have observed in recent years. It isn't led by a big organisation or famous preacher, but increasingly I am meeting young leaders who have been called by God away from the obvious path for them – perhaps they were being lined up to take on a large church from its founder, or had been 'talent spotted' by a leader of a prominent organisation. But they have found themselves leaving the comfort of the clear path and going to places of apparent obscurity, not just for a gap year but to lay down their lives and ambitions for the people they have been called to serve. They find themselves not quite knowing what to do, where they are heading, lacking a five-year plan, but knowing that this is where God has led them.

My prayer is that the story I tell here, which includes the stories that are unfolding in these places, will not only help those following this call to the margins, but will also be inspiring and challenging to anyone who dares to say to God, 'Here am I. Send me' (Isaiah 6:8).

Chapter One
Tohu and *Bohu*

The Bible begins with the Hebrew word *B'reshith*, which we translate as 'In the beginning' (Genesis 1:1). Out of nothing, the God who had no beginning brings the creation into being. The creator God sees what could be, and speaks it into being. The same God who created everything from nothing now lives within us, His people. We should expect that God will give us the ability to see what could be, in people and places where there seems to be nothing. The God who makes a space for life to flourish gives us a creative ability to make space where new life can come.

I remember when I first met one family on our estate. They turned up to one of our Sunday church gatherings, a dad and his two kids. The little girl ran wildly around the room, and her brother hid behind her dad, who was loud, talkative and proceeded to tell us about all the people we knew who he hated, including people who were there that Sunday!

In that moment I had this picture in my head of the three of them lost in worship, singing songs to Jesus and pouring out their love for Him. It was so unexpected and sudden, I knew I couldn't just have made it up. God was

33

showing me His intention for them – out of apparently nothing, God wanted to draw them into a transformative relationship with Him. So far, we have seen one of the children give their life to Jesus and some fulfilment of that picture as they have learned the joy of worshipping Jesus, and we continue to pray for the other two. God brings something out of nothing. A new beginning.

The second verse of the Bible tells us that 'the earth was formless and empty'. The Hebrew language uses the words *tohu* and *bohu*. *Tohu* was often used to describe a wilderness or a deserted city – something that has gone to waste, or is void and empty. Old Testament scholar John Walton says that *tohu* describes 'a situation in which positive values such as purpose and worth are lacking'.[1] *Bohu* can mean void or darkness. The earth was a desert and a wasteland. And we read that 'darkness was over the surface of the deep' (Genesis 1:4). Commenting on the word '*t'hom*', which we translate as 'deep', theologian Karl Barth explains that this primeval, chaotic sea was seen as something to be feared, stating that 'nothing good can come out of *t'hom*'.[2]

This is where the creation of the world begins. In a wilderness and wasteland. In a place of chaos and disorder. 'Nothing good can come out of *t'hom*.' Does that sound familiar to you? It reminds me of Nathanael's comment about Jesus' home town: 'Nazareth! Can anything good come from there?' (John 1:46). The creation of the world begins in a desert, a wasteland, a place of

[1] John Walton, *NIV Cultural Backgrounds Study Bible* (Grand Rapids, MI: Zondervan, 2016), p4.
[2] Karl Barth, *Church Dogmatics III.2* (London: T&T Clark, 2009), p105.

darkness and chaos. This is where God begins. This is where many of us are finding ourselves led by Jesus.

When we first moved into Langworthy, all those words had been applied to the place. It felt empty – a third of the houses were boarded up, left behind by people who couldn't cope with living there any more. There was darkness and chaos – *t'hom* – a lawlessness that created fear. I remember talking to an old school friend who said, 'Langworthy? Why would anyone want to move in there?' It was like a wilderness; it felt like a physical and spiritual desert. It was lacking in positive values such as purpose and worth. There was *tohu* and *bohu* and *t'hom*.

But there is more to it than this. The writer of Genesis tells us:

the Spirit of God was hovering over the waters.[3]

Imagine a long pause before this line is read. Over the darkness, over the chaos, over the fear, over the pain, over the apathy… the Spirit hovers. There is this brooding, this anticipation of new life. Despite the chaos, the darkness and emptiness, there is a more important reality – the brooding presence of the Spirit of God. We are awaiting the Word that brings life.

It seems to me that there is a gift given by God that enables us, amid the chaos and darkness, to sense the brooding of the Spirit, to anticipate the new life that is about to be unleashed – an awareness of the heavenly realm, like Elisha praying for his servant's eyes to be opened when all he could see were the enemy soldiers,

---

[3] Genesis 1:2.

enly the servant could see the angels protecting
ings 6:17-20). It's like Ezekiel looking at a valley
nes and seeing the army that was about to be
raised up (Ezekiel 37:1-14).

Others will dismiss it, but you sense the brooding of the
Spirit. It irritates you inside, like a fire burning in your
bones (Jeremiah 20:9). You can sense words forming
within you that must emerge. Then the words come: 'Let
there be light' (Genesis 1:3).

Words of light and life and order and beauty are
spoken into the chaos and formlessness and darkness.
There is a permission given for the emergence of creativity
and beauty: 'Let there be', not, 'There must be' –
permission rather than coercion. Let them be – release
them to grow, to fly, to swim, to laugh, to build, to love, to
be beautiful – to express the creativity of the Creator. In
this explosion of goodness (the Hebrew word 'tov'), the
darkness and chaos are pushed back and nothing will be
the same again. We need to pray for more explosions of
goodness in our communities, pushing back the darkness,
bringing order to the chaos, blazing a trail of hope and
new life.

We need to call out the goodness. Often when people
visit us in Langworthy, they ask, 'How do we identify the
needs of the area we are moving into?' This is an
important question, but a more exciting question to ask is,
'How can we identify and call out the goodness and
gifting and creativity in this place?' How can we speak
words in Jesus' name and with His authority that explode
with goodness and new life?

Years ago, as we prayed for our estate, we would sing
a song of both lament and hope, which was a prayer for

Langworthy, a prophetic call to rise up again, referring to our estate as a place of beauty.[4] A place once described by a prominent local police officer as a 'sink estate' with 'feral youths' was not seen that way by the Creator. As His people, it was part of our role to speak His words of life and new creation, and to call out the true identity of the estate and its people. Look for the good, name it and call it out. Even if it is something tiny, the size of a 'man's hand' (1 Kings 18:44), pray it into being.

There is so much to glean from these early chapters of Genesis, but there is one other line I want to focus on. We learn in 2:8 that God had 'planted a garden'. This theme of God as a planter, as a gardener, runs throughout Scripture. We learn that God plants His people in the land (Amos 9:15), and there is a longing for a return to this first garden, Eden, in the writings of the prophets; for example:

> The LORD will surely comfort Zion …
> he will make her deserts like Eden,
> her wastelands like the garden of the LORD.
> (Isaiah 51:3)

In 1 Corinthians 3:9 Paul describes the church as 'God's field'.

The same God who plants a garden in Eden will also gather all the nations together in the garden city in the New Creation. It is interesting that in John's Gospel, an account of the New Creation that starts with the phrase, 'In the beginning…' (John 1:1), the author describes the

---

[4] James Gregory (1975-), 'Arise and Shine', https://open.spotify.com/track/14lp3cge4Tz8UfuoCriexT?si=m9BFzy-wTl6nyjxVhtvAfw (accessed 4th January 2022).

first appearance of the risen Jesus in a garden (John 19:41; 20:11-18). In fact, Mary mistakes Him for a gardener! She was actually right. The One who planted her people in the land centuries earlier, the One who planted a garden in Eden in the beginning, the One who will one day oversee the healing of the nations as they eat from the tree of life (Revelation 22:1-5), was standing in front of her in that moment.

The One who spoke the words, 'Let there be light,' into the chaos and confusion of the *tohu* and *t'hom* now speaks directly to her, right at the start of the New Creation. Mary of Magdala, crushed by grief and confusion, now hears the Voice that called the worlds into being, calling her name.

Mary.

She is the first to hear this voice, this voice that brings a new hope, this ancient-future voice that said, 'Let there be light,' and which now brings into the world a new and dazzling light. In this garden of death and grief, heaven and earth are once again united together as in the age-old dream of Eden. On this day heaven and earth come together in this One who stands before her, calling her name. Mary is chosen as the apostle to the apostles, the first preacher of the message that would utterly change the world forever. This is the announcement that the Garden of Eden is being planted once again, that a New Creation has begun.

God is a gardener. And He encourages his people to 'plant gardens' too (Jeremiah 29:5). His image bearers are to be wise stewards of the creation, representing the heavenly Gardener as we pray for His kingdom to come on earth as in heaven. As we plant churches and pioneer into new places, we are reflecting our Creator.

I have reflected on this metaphor of planting. We often use it to describe the first part of a new church or initiative. We plant a church seed, and a church grows up. But planting a garden in an estate context seems different from this, less predictable, more of a genuine step into the unknown. Formulas don't seem to work as they might do in other settings.

We started Langworthy Community Church (LCC) more than eighteen years ago, but I still sometimes say that we are planting a church. Some friends correct me when I say this, and remind me, 'You're just leading a church.'

This is technically true but is not adequate. When you're pioneering in marginalised areas and groups, there is a real sense in which you are always planting. Or maybe there's a better word for it. It's not like you put a seed in the ground, give it all the right conditions and it does exactly what you think it should. It's more like you've got a seed but you don't know what kind of seed it is. An oak tree? A willow? A rose? And the place you've planted it is not known for any kind of growth. So, you're constantly trying out different techniques to help it thrive. Some of them work; some don't. You move it around a bit, it flourishes for a while but suddenly needs a radical change. Then all the leaves fall off and you think it's dead. But then they return more beautiful than ever. You're still not sure what it's becoming, and whether it'll still be there in the morning.

Each stage brings new challenges. Growth and decline, fruit that tastes great, some fruit that goes rotten and you can't explain why. And there's no one who can fully tell you what to do, because the garden is unique. There isn't an Alan Titchmarsh of church planting to tell you exactly when to prune and when to leave it alone. You learn to appreciate the beauty but also that there is no technique that works for more than a season. You have to carefully watch what is growing up, and respond to what is happening now, using what you know but with humility and openness.

So this is why, eighteen years on, I still use the language of planting. It is a long, patient process and nothing can be taken for granted. There are models of planting with much clearer systems and results and even timings, but we need a language that helps those who are planting with unknown seeds into arid soil. We know the seed of the gospel will produce fruit, but we don't know exactly how it will grow up in each place. Or, to use another analogy, we don't know what kind of song will emerge – quoting the ground-breaking Catholic missionary Vincent Donavan:

> When the gospel reaches a people where they are, their response to that gospel is the church in a new place, and the song they will sing is that new, unsung song, that unwritten melody that haunts all of us.[5]

I've spent eighteen years planting in one place, and we are still doing that now. Trying to play our part in seeing the seeds of hope, love, joy, peace and resurrection grow across our estate. It's hard graft at times, but I wouldn't

---

[5] Vincent Donovan, *Christianity Rediscovered* (London: SCM Press, 2019), pxiv.

want to be anywhere else. It is a joy and an honour to join in God's work in the world in this way.

The hope and beauty in the first two chapters of the Bible are the grand entrance to the Scriptures. Imagine a huge medieval cathedral. It has its origins at one point in history, then in different eras new sections have been added – a magnificent entrance, an intricate and private side chapel, a towering spire. But now it stands as one vast building. It is like this with the Bible. Written over approximately 1,000 years, by more than forty different people, it comes to us as one magnificent work of art, bringing us into the presence of God and telling the story of his interactions with people. Genesis 1–2 is the entrance, drawing our gaze upwards at the glory and majesty of it all, setting the themes of what we will discover as we proceed, awestruck, into this place of encounter with the Holy.

After the awe of Genesis 1–2, Genesis 3–11 bring us crashing down to earth with an uncompromising series of stories illustrating what happens when we rebel against God. This is what some theologians call the Fall – when humanity chose to go their own way, the innocence of Eden was lost and a veil was established between heaven and earth. No longer would God be described as 'walking in the garden in the cool of the day' (Genesis 3:8). Adam and Eve are banished from the garden and a sequence of disasters are set in motion.

After the rebellion of Eden, we learn about the first murder (4:8), and the vengeance of Lamech (4:24). Then the ecological disaster of the Great Flood (chapters 6–9), when the evil of humankind was so great that God 'regretted that he had made human beings' (6:6). This

41

depressing section ends with the story of the tower of Babel (chapter 11), finishing in more division and judgement on the people of the earth.

These great stories are sometimes dragged into historical debates. Are they myths? Are they parables? Are they trying to tell us something that actually happened, or some deeper truths? Much more important than debates about whether they *happened* is the fact that they describe what *happens.* Rebellion, jealousy, murder, ecological disaster, revenge, arrogance. You just need to read a newspaper to see that these stories explain to us what happens when humankind rejects the Creator and does its own thing.

This section provides us with insight into the human condition – the darkness within. It holds up a mirror to each generation and we see ourselves staring back, confused and alone. And yet, even within this bleak section of the Bible, there is still hope. There is the righteousness and courage of people like Noah, willing to obey God, and Enoch who 'walked faithfully with God' (5:22). There is the creativity and innovation of Jubal and Tubal-Cain (4:21-22), and, just before the end of the section, we are introduced to a man called Abram.

Chapter Two
Abram and Sarai

Recently I had the privilege of leading the funeral of a friend of ours called Gordon. He was a local legend. An ex-Marine born in the early 1930s, he fought in the Suez crisis and became close friends with the artist Harold Riley. Gordon was a good artist himself, as well as being a talented musician with a liking for jazz and boogie-woogie. Gordon would entertain us all with his stories, music and art. When we first met him, he told us he was sixty, despite being in his mid-seventies at the time! He lived on his own, began to find a sense of community with us, and started attending our Sunday church gatherings.

One Friday night at an Arts Café evening at our LifeCentre community hub, Gordon had an experience that changed him. He said to me, 'I've just been sitting there for the last hour with this feeling I've not had for years, and I've just worked out what it is. I'm happy!' He remembered the previous Sunday when I had described what can happen when God fills us with His Spirit. He said, 'I think that just happened to me!'

I will never forget that following Sunday, when he first took communion at Langworthy Community Church. He said to me afterwards that he had always thought he wasn't good enough for God, that his past ruled him out. But I told him that Jesus invites everyone to His table, and he responded to Jesus' invitation. I remember standing there with tears in my eyes, watching our little church stand to come and share and receive the bread and wine. Instead of Gordon putting his hand up at a preacher's request to give his life to Jesus, with all eyes closed and heads bowed, he stood and came with all of us – hungry, thirsty, broken, all coming to Jesus' table not because of our worthiness but because of our hunger. That is the beauty of Jesus – we are all invited. He puts the lonely in a family (Psalm 68:6).

Gordon realised he could be forgiven and have a fresh start, and told me, 'I finally feel like I belong.' Now he belongs forever to Jesus, experiencing the fullness of the joy, peace and love that he felt on that day.

One thing that Gordon and I agreed on was that it's never too late to start again. Whatever age you are, whatever you have done in your life, whatever has been done to you, you are welcomed by Jesus into His glorious kingdom. Gordon found that in his eighties. He came to church a few weeks later with a huge painting he had created with Jesus on the cross in the middle and biblical scenes all around. As he shared about his experiences of God's presence with him when he had painted it, I realised after around twenty minutes that the talk that I had prepared for that day would have to be binned and God had invited Gordon as our preacher instead!

You might think you're past it, or beyond the pale. You might think you are not good enough for God, or you have messed up too many times. It is *never* too late. No one is too old, too useless, too sinful for God. This is what we learn in the next story, when we are introduced to Abram and Sarai.

After the darkness of the Fall in Genesis 3–11, it is time for a new start. The God who said, 'Let there be light,' now effectively says, 'Let there be a group of people who will be a light in the world.' The God who called the whole of the creation into being now makes a new call. This is a fresh start for humanity. It is the creation of a people who will blaze with the fire of God in a dark and cold world.

Of all the people on the earth at the time, God chose Abram and Sarai to produce the family who would become a nation that would be a blessing to all the families of the earth. A good-looking, healthy couple in their mid-twenties with their whole lives ahead of them, both from successful families, with excellent character and a high capacity, Abram and Sarai were the obvious choice of their time.

Just in case you don't know the story, that last paragraph is not true. In fact, it is the very opposite of the truth. God doesn't seem to recruit people based on their CV, or their character, competence or chemistry. This couple who have been chosen to change the world are old – Abram is seventy-five and Sarai is not far behind. This couple – who have been chosen to produce descendants who will show the world a glimpse of God's kingdom – have no children, and are many years past childbearing age.

Remember where God starts in the creation story of Genesis 1? You could rename Abram and Sarai Mr and Mrs *Tohu-Bohu*. They are past it. Getting their old-age pension. They are barren – a desert and a wasteland. Written off. Or at least, that is how they would have been

45

viewed by many. The writer of Hebrews tells us that Abram was 'as good as dead' (11:12)! Sarai would have lived under the shame of being seen as inadequate or even cursed because of being unable to have children. Abram, whose name means 'Exalted Father', had no one to call him father.

Surely this is something that God calls us all to – to go to the people who have been written off, those who were forgotten about or not noticed by others, those left alone or ignored, to the barren desert, and from a place of prayer to position ourselves for the Spirit to speak through us the words of new creation – 'Let there be…'

This reminds me of the story of St Aidan as told by Bede in *A History of the English Church and People*.[6] In AD635 Aidan was sent from Iona off the west coast of Scotland to Lindisfarne in Northumberland, at the request of King Oswald who wanted him to evangelise the barbaric northerners.

But he wasn't the first missionary to the badlands of the north. Bede reports that there had been another monk before Aidan (of 'a more austere disposition'!) who had tried and failed, and reported to the Ionian monks that the northerners were 'an uncivilised people of an obstinate and barbarous temperament'.[7]

That is seemingly what stirred Aidan into action. The chance to go where others had failed. To minister in a place of wilderness and barrenness, and even danger – but to go with a different spirit. Instead of attempting

---

[6] Bede, *A History of the English Church and People* (Harmondsworth: Penguin Books Ltd, 1955).
[7] Ibid, p146.

conversions through the local rulers, Aidan went to the common people, not riding a horse (a symbol of power) but walking among the people, listening to them and sharing the gospel with gentleness and humility.

And because of that mission, we are here today. The gospel spread like wildfire throughout the north of England, through Aidan, and Hild in the great monastery in Whitby, and then Cuthbert and Herbert and others. It began with a man willing to go to the wilderness and devote himself to a life of prayer, community, listening and mission.

You can see this throughout the Scriptures – God calling the most unlikely ones – the new things starting in the unexpected places and people. And we get all of that in the first twelve chapters of the Bible! Abram and Sarai say yes to God, somehow looking beyond what they can see with their eyes and what they have experienced for many difficult decades, and imagine a different future – a new possibility.

In a society where everything was built around the rhythms of nature, where people believed in a great Wheel of Life and each generation copied the ways of the last one, round and round forever, God called this couple into the unknown – to step into something genuinely new. God called Abram and Sarai to leave behind the most essential sources of their identity as residents of the Ancient Near East: 'Go from your country, your people and your father's household to the land I will show you' (Genesis 12:1). Owning land gave security and prestige. Family ('your people') provided the most basic and fundamental sense of identity. They were called to leave all these things and launch into the unknown – putting their security, identity and future in God's hands. They had to imagine an alternative future. They were even renamed for their new calling – Abraham and Sarah.

This can be one of the biggest challenges in mission on the margins – helping people to imagine a new possibility, to break out of a rut or a generational cycle that traps them. In my first book,[8] I told the story of a friend of ours in Salford whose ambition as a fourteen-year-old was to get pregnant in her final year of school so she could get a council house and live off benefits. When she met Jesus, her imagination was awakened and she went on to excel academically and became an author and teacher. This is what can happen when Jesus interrupts our lives in that wonderful way. The Holy Spirit sanctifies our minds and brings fresh hope and expectation.

Thomas and Claudia lead a fantastic church in Stenhouse in Edinburgh. They took a small team to revitalise a tiny and struggling congregation in 2016, and have been serving that community ever since. Claudia was walking through their estate once when she saw one of the young people who had started to attend their church jumping on a hedge of someone's garden. Claudia decided to ignore it and walked past, but then a few minutes later the boy came running after her, very upset. The owner of the house with the hedge had come out and shouted very aggressively at the boy, scaring and upsetting him. She spoke with the boy about the need to apologise for his own behaviour.

Claudia decided to go and speak to the neighbour with the hedge, partly because she felt guilty about not telling

---

[8] Chris Lane, *Ordinary Miracles* (Watford, Herts: Instant Apostle, 2017).

the boy herself to stop damaging his property, but also because she wanted to challenge the man about his own behaviour towards the child. Slightly intimidated by the man's size and aggression, she knocked on his door anyway. She apologised for her own lack of action, but before she could challenge his reaction, he interrupted by saying how guilty he felt about his excessive anger.

Claudia arranged for the two of them to meet a couple of days later. The young boy was very nervous as they walked up to the man's house, but as soon as the man came out, he got on his knees in front of the boy, saying, 'I'm so sorry for how angry I was; please forgive me. If you ever need anything, you know where to come.' The boy was now utterly shocked as well as feeling nervous, and stuttered his own apology!

This was a moment when a stranger became a friend. It is also a great example of two other things.

First, Claudia's actions enabled both parties to imagine a different outcome. She was brave to challenge the behaviour of others but also to lead by example in confessing her own failings. This opened a door for reconciliation and relationship, rather than perpetuating the negative image of young people in that community and further alienating them from the other residents.

Second, it is a great example of how much we learn from others. Claudia could never have imagined that scene of the intimidating, aggressive neighbour choosing to kneel down in front of a boy who had been damaging his property, and bringing about an alternative future of hope rather than division. She had the courage to knock on that door, but God had even more than she could have imagined in store for them that day. 'All this is from God, who reconciled us to himself through Christ and gave us the ministry of reconciliation' (2 Corinthians 5:18).

This is the beauty of joining in the mission of God – as we step out in acts of courage, helping others to imagine a different future, if we are willing to keep our ears and eyes open, God will then stretch our imaginations too. The coming of the kingdom is always so much better than anything we can ask or imagine!

This is about imagination, but also about obedience. Hebrews 11:8 tells us that Abraham, 'obeyed and went, even though he did not know where he was going'. Referring back to my earlier analogy of the unknown seed, it is not always possible (or desirable) to make five-year plans. Abram, when he left everything behind, *did not know where he was going.* This is so important to remember, especially when we find ourselves in a church culture that uses business models based on three-, five- and ten-year plans which include all kinds of projections of numerical and financial growth, leadership development plans and much more. God often calls us to go into the unknown. This is the true pioneer calling – which depends much more on obedience than on a careful strategy.

Imagine if you had asked Abram about his plan: 'Well, I am going to leave behind everything that gives me security and identity, and go to… a place.'

'Which place, Abram?'

'Erm, a place that God will show me.'

'And what will you do when you get there?'

'Well, I think I might become a great nation and eventually be a blessing to all the families of the earth, but I realise that doesn't look very likely right now.'

'And how will you get to that point? What are your goals?'

'Well, I am going to trust God and keep praying and listening to what He says, and obeying Him.'

'Well, that's not very measurable, is it?'

(Later) 'OK, so Isaac has arrived, this is amazing! What will you do now?'

'Well... me and the boy are going up the mountain together to... worship.'

This is often the nature of the call of God, calling us ever onwards, away from our securities and comforts, beyond our common sense, into a relationship of obedience. As we obey, we learn new things about God.

This is exactly what happens in the disturbing story of Genesis 22. God tells Abraham to sacrifice Isaac – the miracle child – the fulfilment of twenty-five years of waiting and hoping and praying. Abraham obeys and yet still keeps faith in God's promise – believing in resurrection, as we are told in Hebrews 11:19. As father and son go up the mountain together, the son carries the wood for the sacrifice on his back (22:6). Paul tells us in Galatians 3:8 that Abraham was given, 'the gospel in advance'.

Perhaps this story is one of the moments Abraham glimpsed the gospel in advance. Think of the story of Jesus being crucified. The Son ascending the hill, carrying the wood for the sacrifice on His shoulders. The Father believing for resurrection. And then Isaac asks his dad, 'where is the lamb for the sacrifice?' (22:7, GNT). From Mount Moriah, where they were standing, you can see over towards a smaller hill that would come to be known as Calvary. In my mind I picture Abraham looking over in that direction, being given 'the gospel in advance' as he says the words, 'God himself will provide the lamb' (22:8).

Before Abraham is able to carry out this unthinkable act, God stops him and provides an alternative sacrifice. Abraham receives again the promise that through him and his descendants, all the families of the earth will be blessed (Genesis 22:17-18).

What did Abraham learn through this obedience? He learned about the character of God. He learned that God is not like the other 'gods' of the time, who encouraged child sacrifice and were fickle and unpredictable. This is no local god needing to be appeased by horrific acts, but the God of the whole earth whose desire is friendship with humankind and whose intention is to bless the whole earth.

Time and time again God calls us into the unknown. There is always an invitation to break out of the great Wheel of Life, or whichever cycle we are trapped in. There is always a chance to learn more about this endlessly fascinating God who calls us into new adventures. Our obedience always leads to revelation. Obeying God is often uncomfortable and challenging. It often involves us swallowing our pride. It also involves patience.

I find myself spending a lot of time with pioneers and church planters, which is a great joy for me, to be with such creative and passionate people. One trait that is rarer among pioneers is patience! I meet many people who want it all, and they want it *now*. They find themselves kicking against whatever institution they find themselves in, constantly frustrated at the slow pace of their church or denomination, feeling trapped and hemmed in by the lack of progress. It is helpful when they discover that this frustration is one of the shadow sides of the pioneer calling, and that we have a choice about what we do with our frustration. We can let it crush us. We can let it poison our relationships and strike out on our own. Or we can turn that energy into something creative that brings new ideas and teaches us about trust in God.

Abraham is one of the great biblical pioneers. He receives a clear promise from God about having a son. After that promise he has to wait for twenty-five years until he sees it come to pass! Imagine him on his eightieth birthday, wondering when it will happen, whether he imagined it all. He turns ninety and still no child. He blows out ninety-five candles, he's not getting any younger...

Imagine having a clear promise from God, including an angelic visitation, but then seeing no sign of the answer for all those years! Imagine Abraham's thoughts on this: 'Did I hear correctly? Maybe it is a metaphorical myriad of descendants? Maybe I need to make it happen myself?' Ishmael is the result of Abraham trying to make the promise happen himself, with all the pain involved in that story (Genesis 16).

There are many people holding on to promises from God for their communities. In Langworthy there are a number of big dreams we have that we haven't seen come to pass yet. One of our big dreams has been to see many young people come to know Jesus for themselves. We have seen some, but nowhere near what we long to see. We have believed that God wants to bring whole families to faith all over the estate. Again, we have seen some of this, but we are miles away from what we originally dreamed about. It feels as though God has given us little signs and glimpses, just enough for us to continue hoping and praying.

It seems to me that one of the keys to pioneering in estate contexts like Langworthy is that we learn to live in the space between the glorious vision we are working towards and the often difficult reality that we see with our eyes. And this requires patience. In *The Patient Ferment of the Early Church*,[9] Alan Kreider identifies patience of one of the most important factors in the growth of the earliest church. Patience is certainly something we have had to learn over the years.

When we moved into Langworthy in 1999, amid much fanfare and prayer, coming off the back of the prayer movements and spiritual renewal in the 1990s in the UK, I was pretty convinced we were going to see a massive revival across the estate within a few weeks. We had a large team who were talented and passionate, we were backed by incredible financial and practical support from our friends at The Message Trust, and God had spoken to us in remarkable ways about what we were called to do here. Cultivating patience was the least of my concerns.

It was all in place – the team, the support, the prayer. We were reminded that lots of the great revivals happened in the poorest areas. All the factors were there. 'If my people, who are called by my name, will humble themselves and pray and seek my face and turn from their wicked ways, then I will hear from heaven, and I will forgive their sin and will heal their land' (2 Chronicles 7:14). We did a lot of praying, a lot of repenting and

---

[9] Alan Kreider, *The Patient Ferment of the Early Church* (Grand Rapids, MI: Baker Academic, 2016).

turning from our wicked ways in those days! We humbled ourselves in fasting, and then asked God to heal our land.

We saw some young people come to faith, and some of their families too. We saw crime and antisocial behaviour decrease consistently each year. People began to move back into an estate that was once deserted by a third of its residents. There are many stories of hope and beauty. Have we seen revival? No, at least not at all how we imagined it to be. Not like the books about Azusa Street or the Hebrides. People became disillusioned and tired. We were the revival generation – or so we had been told in soaring sermons and anthemic songs. We wanted to see hundreds of young people come to faith. We wanted to see miraculous healings on a daily basis, and people in every household giving their lives to following Jesus.

As I type this, sitting in my garden shed on a cold January afternoon, I think back more than two decades to January 1999. I was twenty-three years old with a full head of hair, and about to make the move into Langworthy. I was engaged to be married, although Esther and I hadn't told anyone yet. Manchester United were in the middle of their historic treble-winning season. Some people were stockpiling tins of food in their basements in case the 'Millennium Bug' plunged the world into chaos. Some of my current closest friends hadn't even entered my life yet. I wonder what my twenty-three-year-old self would think of what has happened? Or what I would think of what *hasn't* happened?

I wonder if my twenty-three-year-old self would still have moved into Langworthy if I had known that twenty-two years later we wouldn't yet have seen the kind of transformation we had been dreaming about then. Like

Abraham, would I have been willing to go to a place and wait for decades for the promises to be fulfilled? How patient are we as we live in the gap between what we long for and what we see in reality? Our hearts long ultimately for the new creation – a restoration of Eden; heaven and earth united together again – so in reality we will always live with this aching chasm until Jesus returns. But God is kind to us and He gives us glimpses of our hearts' desires. He walks with us in the barren years, He visits us and reminds us of His promises, just like the three visitors do for Abraham and Sarah (Genesis 18).

Just like Zacchaeus who is transformed as he provides hospitality to Jesus (Luke 19:1-10), Abraham and Sarah receive a reminder of the promise – and the breakthrough they have longed for – as they provide hospitality for the three visitors. Abraham received hospitality earlier from the mysterious Melchizedek, King of Salem, who blessed him and gave him bread and wine (Genesis 14:18-20), and now, as he provides food and welcome for these representatives of God, all those years of waiting will begin to reach their fulfilment. I find it interesting how Sarah laughs (Genesis 18:12). After all these years, after all the pain and disappointment, will it really happen now? And the child who fulfils the promise is named Isaac – which means, 'he laughs' (Genesis 21:3, 6).

In the past couple of years, which have probably been the most painful for us as a church, I have never laughed so much. Laughter helps us to get rid of negative emotions and replaces them with a sense of hope. Laughter unites the group who are sharing the moment. You can't laugh properly unless you are at ease with the others in the room, certainly not the kind of belly laughing where your whole body shakes and you think you might die if you don't stop soon! It is like a gift from God that He gives us to help us in the darkest moments, to laugh at how ludicrous life often is, but also to start afresh and believe again that the impossible might actually happen.

There are moments in all our lives when we are given these glimpses of heaven – in hilarious laughter with friends, or in bread and wine given to us, or in a word spoken by a stranger.

As we conclude this section on Abraham and Sarah, it is worth reflecting on how much there is to learn from their story. These pioneers of faith were too old, barren and sometimes made the wrong choices, and yet this is where God chose to create a community of people who would be a light in a dark world. This is the couple who were selected to produce a great nation who would be a blessing to all the families of the earth. These are the brave and patient pioneers who were given the gospel in advance. As we step into the unknown in obedience to our own callings, and wrestle with the gap between our dreams and the reality we see with our eyes, let us be inspired by this story of patience, hope and new life springing out of the most unexpected places.

Chapter Three
Moses and Miriam

I was standing in a hospital ward, exhausted and elated. My wife, Esther, had just given birth to our third child. Esther was arguably rather more tired than I was, although as all men know, childbirth is tough for us blokes, all that encouraging and hand-holding. We had decided to call the baby Hannah, but hadn't thought of a middle name. The moment I first held her in my arms I said 'Miriam'. Into my mind came this courageous leader who at a young age had saved the life of her baby brother, Moses. Miriam was one of the three people chosen by God to lead the people out of slavery in Egypt, along with her brothers, Moses and Aaron (Micah 6:4). Jewish tradition says that as Moses led the men out of slavery and taught them the law, Miriam did the same for the women. She led the people in singing to the God who frees the slaves and who topples the powerful rulers (Exodus 15:21).

As I held this fragile new life in my arms, I was struck by the potential in each new baby. Miriam began her life in the same way, and went on to be considered to be one of the seven great female prophets in Judaism, inspiring and leading a whole nation in worship, and being ranked alongside her brothers in leading the most significant event in her nation's history. I prayed for my little Hannah Miriam, that she too would follow the way of God and lead many others to do so.

Miriam had to live much of her life in the shadow of her little brother, Moses. I guess she didn't call him 'Ar Kid' like we do in Salford, but we have no evidence either way. My little brother eclipsed me in a number of ways, but mostly in sports. I will never forget playing him at tennis when he was thirteen and I was seventeen, and he very nearly beat me. I was so disturbed by this that I resolved to never play him at any sport again! Andrew went on to become better than me at every sport we both played, much to my displeasure, and eventually I swallowed my pride and we played tennis again. I don't feel that I need to share the result with you.

Miriam's little brother Moses' life is fascinating, and has been the focus of many feature films and novels. After escaping death as a baby, he grows up in a royal palace and is raised as a prince by the pharaoh's family. Then, after killing an Egyptian in a fight, he flees to the desert and becomes a sheep farmer in Midian.

It is here that he hears the voice of God calling him to return to Pharaoh with a message to free his people from slavery. As the book of Exodus progresses, it follows a dramatic sequence of judgement with the ten plagues, and the eventual escape from Egypt, across the Red Sea into freedom, then to Mount Sinai to receive the covenant from God.

This story is so important in the big story of Scripture for several reasons. First, it is the time when the people of God become a nation. Through the story of Joseph (the lad with the colourful coat and offensive dreams), the twelve families of Israel (Israel who used to be called Jacob, the son of Isaac, son of Abraham) ended up living in Egypt. These twelve families reproduced rather rapidly: they were fruitful *and* multiplied greatly *and* became exceedingly numerous (Exodus 1:7), and became the twelve tribes of Israel, a significant enough presence to be considered a threat to the pharaoh. But it is only when they emerge from their slavery that the *tribes* of Israel become the *nation* of Israel.

The Exodus is also significant because it is the time when the people receive the covenant from God, a whole way new of living that sets them apart from the surrounding nations, as God's chosen people. Also important in this time is the fact that God shares his name with them – YHWH – which means 'I am who I am'. Each school year, there is always a day when one of my kids comes home giggling because they have found out the first name of their new teacher; she isn't just 'Mrs Jones' any more – she is 'Jackie'! They spotted her full name on a letter, and they feel that they know her as a person now, not just as a teacher. When the Most High God shares His name with Moses, it is a sign of a new closeness between God and the people.

The Exodus is also important for Christians, not just for the reasons already listed, but also because Jesus Himself uses the word to describe His own mission. In that strange scene on the Mount of Transfiguration, Jesus is talking to Moses and Elijah, and Jesus tells the Exodus man – Moses – about the *Exodus* that He is going to accomplish (Luke 9:30-31). Not just for one nation at one point in history, but for the whole world – a freedom from sin and oppression and all kinds of evil, and ultimately from death.

One of the reasons for immersing ourselves in the grand narrative of the Bible is that we find ourselves relating to different points in the story at different points in our lives. We might find our lives falling apart and relate to the questions and anguish of Job, or sense a call to a great task to which we feel utterly inadequate, and are inspired by the story of Gideon, found in the book of Judges. The story of Moses and Miriam – the great story of the Exodus – is another one of those framing narratives.

One of the reasons I wanted to write this book is because of the truths we learn about from Moses' experience as a desert farmer in Midian. After his privileged upbringing in the royal court, Moses has fled to the desert. I think it is interesting that in the Bible and in Church history, often God reveals the deepest truths in the desert places. In the wilderness. In the *tohu* and *bohu*. On the margins of society. In the most difficult situations when God can seem far away and our purpose for life unclear, often that is where the deepest truths are discovered.

Think of Joseph's statement, 'God has made me fruitful in the land of my suffering' (Genesis 41:52). Or John the Baptist, preaching in the desert, preparing 'the way for the Lord' (Matthew 3:3). Jesus spends His forty days in the desert, overcoming the devil, and emerges 'in the power of the Spirit' (Luke 4:14). Almost all of Jesus' ministry is on the margins of society, away from the big centres and the powerful people. The Desert Fathers and Mothers retreated to the barren places to gain wisdom and to fight spiritual battles. The Celtic saints of the sixth and seventh centuries did likewise.

And here, far away from Egypt, a long way from his ultimate calling, living the life of an anonymous farmer on the far side of the desert of Midian, near the holy mountain of Horeb (which means 'wasteland'), Moses sees a burning bush (Exodus 3). Not an unusual sight in a desert, except that the bush is not burning up. Moses approaches out of curiosity, and in that moment, on the far side of a wilderness in the middle of nowhere, the God who saved him from death as a child now gives him his life's purpose – to rescue His people from slavery in Egypt and lead them into the Promised Land. It will be a long and tortuous process, a calling that will lead them not just out of slavery but then into forty years of desert wanderings. There will be dramatic confrontations with the pharaoh, stunning miracles, tragedies and thrilling escapes, but this moment in the desert, and the subsequent forty years in that same desert, would be the foundation of the self-understanding of the people of God for all the generations to come.

It is in this desert that they are given the covenant. It is in this desert that the manna and quail miraculously appear (Exodus 16). It is here that Moses gets to glimpse the glory of the Lord, in all its awe and wonder and compassion (Exodus 33–34). It is in the desert that they are led by the cloud and the fire. And it is on the edge of the Promised Land, but still in the desert, that Moses dies.

He never got to lead the people into the Promised Land. Did he fail? Or was his Promised Land ultimately not a geographical area but the presence and glory of God, which Moses had longed for and pursued his whole life? Perhaps in that moment when he died, the great goal and calling of his life was fulfilled as he entered fully into the presence of God, in all its glory?

We all have our 'promised land' dreams and goals. In the previous chapter I outlined some of ours in Langworthy. The early church writer Irenaeus of Lyons spoke of the Church being 'planted like the garden of Eden in the world'.[10] I love this phrase – it sparks my imagination. Where God has called you, what would it look like for it to resemble the Garden of Eden? A place of unbroken fellowship with God? A place where the wolf and the lamb can live together (Isaiah 11:6)? The prophet Isaiah saw a time for Israel when God would make 'her deserts like Eden, her wastelands like the garden of the LORD' (Isaiah 51:3). Ezekiel foresaw a day when the desolate land '[had] become like the garden of Eden; the cities that were lying in ruins, desolate and destroyed, are now fortified and inhabited' (Ezekiel 36:35).

We have many dreams for Langworthy. When we moved in, it felt so desolate. Abandoned houses, burnt-out cars, a lack of hope. We want to see the opposite of this. We are praying the prayer that Jesus taught us – let 'your kingdom come, your will be done, on earth as it is in heaven' (Matthew 6:10). The kingdom of God involves peace, love, hope, joy, community, courage, laughter and freedom, all centred on and derived from the King – Jesus.

The full coming of the kingdom of God is the Promised Land that we are all praying for – the restoration of Eden on earth. This is good news for everyone. Imagine what it

---

[10] Irenaeus, *Against Heresies 5.20.2.*,
www.newadvent.org/fathers/0103520.htm (accessed 12th October 2021).

could look like in your community. Write down the words and pictures that come to mind. Pray for these things every day.

I will not get to set foot in that Promised Land in my lifetime. But, like when the spies brought back the grapes from the Promised Land (Numbers 13:23), while we are still in the desert we can taste what the future is like. Claudia in Edinburgh had a taste of that future when her neighbour knelt in repentance on his front lawn. It was a moment of totally unexpected goodness. It was a moment when God answered the ancient prayer and let the kingdom come 'on earth as it is in heaven' – a moment that could be described as 'holy'. A moment to take your shoes off. In the wasteland of Horeb, or in a front garden of a forgotten and neglected estate in Edinburgh, we see a glimpse of the planting of Eden. Holy ground.

If we are attentive to the leading of the Spirit, we find holy ground everywhere.

I encountered it recently in a head teacher's office. As I was a pretty good kid at school, I was never summoned to the head teacher's office. This was good because our head teacher was terrifying! If we saw the head walking towards us, we would instantly check our ties were in place and make sure we could remember how to spell their surname – something they loved to check at random moments! Even now as a forty-six-year-old man, I still check I am wearing the right shoes if I see my ex-head in the street (they live in our neighbourhood), and I rehearse their surname in my mind. In my high school there were two lights on the head's door – red for wait, green for come in. I imagined the room to be like Room 101 from George

Orwell's *1984* – all my worst fears coming together in one place. Fortunately I avoided 'The Summons' to their office.

Nearly thirty years on, I found myself in the office of another head teacher. After the struggles of the year I described at the start of the book, our church was looking to start meeting in public again. We had little money owing to our smaller numbers, so were praying for somewhere to meet at low cost. I wasn't convinced about using this school because it wasn't in the heart of the estate but on the edge. However, as we talked with the head teacher, I started to sense the presence of God. That same presence that I have sensed in big worship meetings, or when receiving prayer ministry, or when we take communion together. But I was in a school office!

In that moment I was convinced that this was where God was leading us. The head teacher welcomed us with overwhelming kindness and generosity, and our partnership and friendship with them and the school has been incredibly fruitful ever since. In Luke 10 Jesus tells His followers to look for the people of peace (Luke 10:6) who will welcome them, to receive their hospitality and then to heal the sick and proclaim that 'the kingdom of God has come near' (vv7-9).

This is what we have been trying to do over the past couple of years – to be a blessing. As we have received kindness and hospitality, we have tried to share the good news of Jesus and provide glimpses for people of that glorious day when there will be no more pain and tears, and death will be swallowed up forever (Isaiah 25:6-8). It is wonderful what God can do through us when we give ourselves fully over to Him.

It is also important to remember that a calling into the desert is not all about what God does *through* us – giving people a glimpse of the Promised Land in all its beauty. It is also about what God does *in* us in the desert. Often we can become so excited by the promises that God gives us for a place or a group of people, that we focus all our thoughts on the transformation that God can achieve in the lives of others – the planting of Eden as we serve, the coming of the *shalom* of God. In doing this we can neglect what is arguably the primary call – for us to be transformed.

My friends Sam and Katy are pioneering church in an estate in Chester called The Groves. They are a very gifted, multitalented couple who have been involved in Christian ministry for many years. Reflecting on their call to this estate, they imagined at first that their mission was to help many people see their lives transformed. But as time went by it became clear to them that 'the call is about going to be with God'. It wasn't about them bringing about change, but about God bringing about change within them.

Referring to the story of Moses, Sam says, 'I don't think you can get this anywhere but the desert. In the desert all scaffolding is stripped away. You never graduate from imperfection, vulnerability and prayer.' I have seen this process develop in their lives over the past few years. It takes great courage to persevere and be shaped by God in this way – to embrace vulnerability as an invitation to be formed into Christlikeness.

In the desert, Moses leaves behind his years of privilege and is prepared for his life's mission. His status and success are taken away as he humbly tends the sheep. When the call eventually comes – a call to free a nation from slavery – any arrogance from his royal past is gone, and Moses asks the question, 'Who am I that I should go…?' (Exodus 3:11).

This is a work that God wants to do in each one of us, and it is often in the desert that it happens. Recently I was at a retreat centre on the south coast of England, and I went for a walk in the grounds. I reached a field where there were some tree stumps to sit on. I was reflecting on how inadequate I was feeling in my calling, how weak and foolish I was, and I was reminding myself of the verse: 'The one who calls you is faithful, and he will do it' (1 Thessalonians 5:24).

My thoughts went back to when I first started out in Christian ministry as a youth worker – the young leaders I had invested in, the worship events we did that would gather large groups of youth from across the region, and the arrogance I had at the time about my 'achievements'. Then I reflected on the past decade or two – such a different experience. Breaking new ground, investing in people with little or no Christian background, often with limited or no obvious 'fruit'. I was keenly feeling the imperfection and vulnerability that Sam refers to.

I noticed some ashes on the grass where a fire had been the night before. Into my head came the phrase, 'Do nothing out of selfish ambition or vain conceit' (Philippians 2:3), and I felt God whisper to me, 'That's what I've been doing with your selfish ambition and vain conceit over the past twenty years – burning it away.' It has been pretty painful! Why did it have to last for twenty years and not forty days? And why is it still ongoing?

I had reached a Moses moment – who am I that I should go? What do I have to offer? I've got nothing!

God's answer to Moses is the same as His answer to each of us when we ask that question: 'I will be with you' (Exodus 3:12). He doesn't say, 'You're awesome! Live your best life now! Be yourself! Nothing can stop you! Everything is going to be OK!' He says, 'I will be with you.'

That is what we need to hear. However you are feeling, whatever the circumstances, this is the stunning, world-changing truth: God will be with you. The call into the desert is a call to be with God, and God will be with us.

Do you notice that God doesn't answer Moses' question? Moses says, 'Who am I?' (Exodus 3:11) – making it about him and his limitations. God answers with the more important truth: 'I will be with you.'

Another friend, also called Sam, said to me of his experience of working in an estate, 'We went in thinking we were saviours.' This is often the case in mission. There is a call from God and we respond, but then we can act as if we are the saviours, whereas there is only one Saviour. We also need to be saved, again and again. Saved from our own selfishness, our arrogance, our addictions. It's what theologians call being 'sanctified'.

Thomas and Claudia describe their experience in Stenhouse as needing to 'get rid of the saviour complex'. For us in Salford, God called us to Langworthy to be with Him. God called us to Langworthy to encounter Him. In what was widely considered to be a desert place, we have met Him time and time again in shopping centres, breakfast groups, food banks and even head teachers' offices. Those places have been like our experience of a burning bush. Something that looks ordinary and yet is somehow different. We needed saving. We needed converting. We have been saved, we are being saved, and we will be saved.

Moses is still unsure: 'What if they do not … listen to me?' (Exodus 4:1). Well, here's some news, Moses: they won't! But you still have to obey, you still have to speak, and God's promises will still be fulfilled.

'But I'm not very good at speaking!' (v10).

'I will help to you speak, Moses!'

'Please send someone else' (v13)!

God is speaking to him out of a burning bush and he still doesn't believe it! But even then, God is gracious and provides Aaron to help him, and the two brothers and their sister, Miriam, lead the people to freedom.

However inadequate you feel, however unsure you may be, however weak or old or 'slow of speech' (v10) you might feel, God will be with you!

One of the key questions God asks in the desert is this one: 'What is that in your hand?'

Moses looks and says, 'A staff' (v2). Just a branch, a bit of wood.

'Throw it on the ground' (v3). It becomes a snake!

'Pick it up' (see v4). It turns back again.

Through this gnarled old shepherd's staff, many miracles will happen over the coming months for Moses. God can use whatever is in our hand. In the desert we learn that God can do miracles even in our weakness and vulnerability.

Here is one example. When I was at high school, my mum wanted to make a difference at my school for God. Not being a youth worker, and actually being smaller than most of the pupils, she decided against offering her services for assemblies and RE lessons. What was in her

69

hand? Well, she could pray. So she formed a prayer group with some other ladies who had a heart for the school. I used to call it the Small Women's Prayer Group, for obvious reasons.

Anyway, one summer, my mum and the other small pray-ers decided to go in and visit the head teacher to ask if there was anything they could pray for. The head teacher explained that what tends to happen during the summer holidays is that some pupils miss school so much that they come back on to the school grounds, but bring BB guns with them and shoot holes in the windows. The previous summer they had had to replace forty-six windows. So the group got on to praying, and when they returned in September, the head teacher was delighted to inform them that no windows had been broken whatsoever!

On another occasion my mum was walking past the school and felt God stir her to pray that he would 'blast the evil out of the school'. I will always remember this day. In the afternoon, a bolt of lightning hit a tree just next to a classroom. Everyone went berserk, and all classes stopped for a while. What we didn't know till later was that in the classroom next to the tree, someone was teaching the class about the occult – séances, Ouija boards and the like. This was the lesson that was disrupted!

Now what can we learn from this? First, you don't mess with my mum. She might be only little, but if you get on the wrong side of her, be careful in a thunderstorm! But my main point is, she used what she had in her hand, and miracles happened.

Each of us has something in our hands, which, when given over to God, can be like the bread and fish that the little boy gave to Jesus and fed 5,000 people (John 6). Miracles in the desert.

God wants to invite each one of us into the desert. It might be for forty days or forty years, or possibly for the rest of our lives. While we are there, it is possible that 'The desert and the parched land will be glad; the wilderness will rejoice and blossom' (Isaiah 35:1). But it might not! Many people might listen and respond. Or they might ignore us! It may be that we just get a taste of some of that fruit from the Promised Land. And that will be enough. Because in the end, we realise that this is ultimately not about our life goals and big dreams, but is a pursuit of the presence of God. And when we reach the end of our lives, our reward is the same as that of Moses: to behold the fullness of the glory of God. May God's kingdom come 'on earth as it is in heaven'.

Chapter Four
Unlikely Leaders

Moses' assistant Joshua led the people across into the Promised Land, with his own 'Moses moment' as the Jordan river dried up to allow them to cross (Joshua 3:14-17). There followed a series of bloody battles as they established themselves in the land, before the eventual death of Joshua. As we read the book of Judges, we come to a liminal moment, in between the two great historical periods of Moses-Joshua and the kingship of Saul, David and Solomon. In this in-between time we discover that the next generation grew up, 'who knew neither the LORD nor what he had done for Israel' (Judges 2:10). In response to this, God raised up a series of judges, or 'saviours' who would call the people back to God, deliver them from their enemies, and bring peace and blessing to the land again. But each time the judge died, the people would stray from God again and judgement would come.

One of the brilliant things about the book of Judges is the collection of people who are chosen to lead and save their nation. Seemingly every one of them is unsuitable for the task, or has some flaw or huge obstacle in their way. It is a collection of the most unlikely people who, despite everything, are chosen by God and bring peace to the people. Jephthah was the son of a prostitute, who was driven out of his family because of his parentage (Judges 11). Gideon was even more unwilling than Moses – an angel appeared to him and he still tried to refuse, claiming that his family was the weakest and he was the weakest member of his family (Judges 6)! Yet God delivered Israel under his leadership against overwhelming odds. Samson was a Nazirite dedicated to the avoidance of alcohol and haircuts, and yet was strangely drawn to both (Judges 13-16)! Yet he, too, saved Israel. And Deborah – this awesome leader who brought a combination of spiritual, military and political leadership – led her people to victory and peace in a fiercely patriarchal world (Judges 4).

All unlikely. Most deeply flawed. Yet God chose them. Just like Abraham and Moses. It is surely no coincidence that Jesus did the same thing when choosing His disciples. He didn't go for the people with the best CV – the most intelligent, the most stable or powerful. He didn't sit down in a plush office and choose His dream team from a list of people with the best chemistry, character and competence.

Jesus began in an unstrategic place with a collection of unlearned fishermen, traitors and terrorists, and invested His life into them. Jesus saw beyond the surface and called out their potential. He forgave, corrected and restored them when they messed up. He trained this ragtag bunch of rejects to heal the sick, preach the gospel and cast out demons. He taught them how to pray and how to trust God for provision. He taught them how to love each other with God's love. He taught them how to engage with the Scriptures and what it meant to embrace those who were different from them.

Often the popular leadership books assume an ability to recruit highly skilled and obviously gifted people who are consistent and stable. But the reality is that the vast majority of the Church don't have that luxury. It would be great to see more books about how to raise up Gideons who have no confidence, or Jephthahs who have been excluded because of their heritage, or Samsons who just keep messing up but still want to serve God. Imagine a seminar where we learn how to run a small group that contains someone who would like to kill tax collectors (Simon the Zealot) *and* an actual tax collector (Levi)! Those Bible studies could be awkward! But this is the work of almost everyone involved in mission and church leadership all over the world, and especially in areas blighted by high levels of crime and poverty.

As always, we turn to the example of Jesus. We should be comforted by the presence of Judas Iscariot in the Twelve. Jesus loved him just as much as He loved the others, and invested in him in the same way. He even honoured him by having him dip his bread in the bowl with Him at the Last Supper (Matthew 26:23). But still Judas betrayed Him. And still Peter denied Him. Still the other disciples ran away and hid when He was arrested.

And yet... this group of eleven deserters are restored and go on to turn the world upside down in Jesus' name. Peter – who is actually called 'Satan' by Jesus Himself (Matthew 16:23) – the only one to explicitly deny Jesus *three* times – it is Peter the denier who stands up in front of that huge crowd on the day of Pentecost to preach that first evangelistic sermon. I love the fact that the first evangelistic sermon in the history of the Church begins with the words, 'We are not drunk' (see Acts 2:15)! The boldness of the apostles makes people think they have been drinking. And the newly restored Peter preaches with courage and clarity; this message of a risen Saviour which cuts to the heart of the listeners is then carried by the pilgrims all over the known world, and the Church is born.

But it isn't just about the eleven. In a world where the testimony of a woman was not considered valid in court, the risen Jesus entrusts the first apostolic mission to Mary Magdalene (John 20:17). It is the women in Jesus' group who help to finance them, and it is the same women who are still there at the cross when most of the disciples have fled.

Jesus continually affirms and includes those who are most devalued and excluded. The Gospel of Luke is a constant stream of examples of how Jesus does this. In the very first chapter we are introduced to Mary, the teenager who is pregnant outside marriage, and to Zechariah, the male priest. Luke puts their stories alongside each other and then subverts the expectations of the day by showing Mary as the example of faithfulness to God, and Zechariah as the one who doubts. In chapter 2 we see the message about the Messiah being first revealed to lowly night shepherds in the fields, and the baby Jesus being affirmed in His calling not by the high priest but by the widow Anna and the old man Simeon. In chapter 3 we begin with a list of all the powerbrokers of that day – the emperor, the tetrarchs and the priests. And it tells us that the word of the Lord goes to… none of them! It goes to John, eating his locusts and wearing his hair shirt. Where? In the desert, of course!

Luke's Gospel just keeps going like this. Among the Gospel writers, only Luke tells us the parable of the Good Samaritan (Luke 10). Only Luke gives us the story of the criminal next to Jesus being granted salvation in his dying moments (Luke 23:43). Luke is quick to point out Jesus' many interactions with women, children, slaves, prostitutes, lepers and other outcasts.

This has echoes of the story of King David when he was in the cave at Adullam, and 400 people who 'were in distress or in debt or discontented gathered round him', and he created a new community for them and became their leader (1 Samuel 22:1-2).

Jesus, often called the Son of David, has the same magnetic effect on all who are marginalised. As they gather around Him and the religious leaders scoff, He 'welcomes sinners, and eats with them' (Luke 15:2), and they accuse Him of being 'a glutton and a drunkard' (Luke 7:34). Jesus creates a new community around a common table, and thus models what the kingdom of God looks like.

Imagine a church plant whose aim it is to go into a desert place and gather 400 people (the number is unimportant) who are in distress or in debt or discontented, and form them into a community of Jesus-followers. Imagine the mess and the beauty that would emerge! May God raise up more Davids to love the distressed and discontented.

This is not just for the talented and stable ones. Not just for the holy and committed. Everyone is invited. Everyone is welcome. Something new is being formed and it is especially for those who have been excluded up to this point. It is for those who keep messing up and are impulsive and unreliable. Pull up a chair, Simon Peter. It is for the hot-headed and ambitious. Have a seat, James and John. It is for those who are too busy and who fall out with their siblings. Welcome, Martha and Mary. Those who think Jesus has lost His mind – you can come too, Mary, James, Jude and the other brothers. There is always more room. We can get out the emergency chairs if we need to. Judas, come and eat, even when you are plotting betrayal. To the nameless lady known only as 'a sinner' (Luke 7:37, NRSVA). Your worship is utterly beautiful, and your name is known to God if not to us. Come and pull up a pew.

Let me tell you a couple of stories of how God chooses the unlikely ones in our day. I had the privilege of meeting Hana about four years ago, as she joined my formation group at college to train for ordination in the Church of England. Hana quickly established herself as a popular and much-loved part of the college community. Incredibly kind, empathetic and with an outstanding gift of encouragement, Hana got on well with everyone and, despite some nerves about the challenge of studying for an MA in Theology, consistently showed an astute and creative theological instinct. If Hana hadn't told me her story I would never have believed it.

As a child, Hana remembers the family relocating after a member of her family was attacked. Eventually her parents split up and both started new families. As she approached her teenage years, Hana suffered some emotional and physical abuse. This left her with a deep longing to be loved, especially by men, and she found herself being drawn into gang culture, and meeting men on the internet, which led to a number of serious sexual assaults.

Eventually Hana got into a very dysfunctional relationship, and ended up sleeping in an airport and being taken in by the police. While living in a grimy, dangerous hostel, Hana realised something had to change. She needed to get out of this relationship and return home.

After a traumatic end to the relationship, Hana sat in her room reflecting on her future. She started to write on the wall, and found that she was writing about Jesus! Then she developed a strong urge to read the Bible. She began at Revelation (author's note: not always the most sensible place to start), and quickly found herself believing in Jesus. Hana describes this process as like a death to her old life – with all the pain that this implies. She instantly found herself with an incredible hunger for God. She found a church and wandered in. As they sang songs to Jesus together, Hana encountered the most beautiful feeling she had ever known, like rain falling all over her – an outpouring of the Holy Spirit.

Learning difficulties meant Hana struggled with reading, so music and worship became a primary source of her spiritual growth, and through the actions and welcome of the church members she found some of the love and acceptance her heart had been yearning for. 'I knew Jesus through the people,' she says.

Things began to move quickly for Hana from this point. Her dad found faith through her, and within three months she was taking part in an overseas mission trip. Hana threw herself into all the church activities she could find, encountering the love of Jesus again and again. She would tell her story of transformation to many people and groups, but after a while her life became difficult again. In her words, 'Sometimes you burn out from being good.' Her story of transformation had become something that had happened in the past and was now tired and old.

After encountering some more difficulties in her life, Hana went from one extreme to the other. Instead of living all out for Jesus, she found herself falling away from church and Christian living in a major way – into a life of 'sex, drugs and drum and bass'. For the first few years of her twenties, Hana only occasionally visited her church, sometimes when drunk, but still in those moments sensed the love of God for her through the people.

In her mid-twenties she had another decisive encounter with God, and from that moment stopped her destructive drug-taking. This time things were different. No longer was the narrative, 'I once was a terrible sinner and now I am complete and whole.' This time it was more nuanced: 'This is me, in my fragility, coming to God.' She felt like Jonah, running in the opposite direction but then being swallowed up and spat out where she was meant to be, bruised and fragile, but in the right place.

Just like her first encounter with God, this return to faith led quickly to action. While experiencing some wonderful healing from the past, she found herself being called to study, and moved up north to Chester. Here she developed a deep love for learning and found the confidence to respond to a sense of calling to train for ordination. She felt God say to her, 'You're going to go to places you've never been before and reach people you've never reached.'

And so began a journey Hana could never have imagined a few years earlier. Seemingly miraculously, she was recommended for training. Hana admits she wouldn't even have recommended herself!

On the day she first began her training, Hana describes walking into a grand, cavernous cathedral and feeling intimidated and out of place. 'I just felt like scum,' is how she puts it. In those early days she was advised to change the way she dressed and talked, and so she tried to change in order to fit in. I remember sitting down with Hana after a few weeks and encouraging her to resist fitting the mould. In seminars about working in inner-city estates, she struggled with the way some people talked about 'reaching the poor and the lost', as if they were a project or even a different type of human.

Over her three years in training, I had the privilege of watching Hana find her place and her own voice. Not trying to conform to someone else's expectations of what a minister-in-training should be like, but bringing all she is to the table, including the difficulties of the past, and, indeed, of the present. I saw what it looks like when someone doesn't try to create a false division in their life – 'I used to be like this, but then I met God and now everything has changed' – but sees God at work at every stage in her life, even in the messiest and darkest times, and acknowledges that there is always some brokenness and more healing that is needed. She has given up on trying to look victorious and righteous, and instead is focusing on what God can do through her in every situation.

I think this is utterly beautiful. When Jesus rose from the dead, He still had the scars of the crucifixion on His hands, feet and side. When He gives resurrection life to us by His Spirit, there are still scars, but they are part of our story.

Hana's story is miraculous, amazing and beautiful. It is also painful, messy and incomplete. When I spend time with her I find it easy to forget what she has been through because of what God has done in her and what God does through her. Hana is now planting a new church, building a team and reaching a new estate with the good news of Jesus. She has completed her MA with Merit and is leading fellow church leaders in reflecting on how we invest in and train up leaders from more unlikely backgrounds.

I absolutely love who Hana is and what she is doing. I love how Jesus shines out of her. She reminds me that I should never write someone off because they don't fit the mould of what I might consider to be a leader. She challenges me to listen deeply to people who are different from me. She reminds me to listen, to always be attentive to what the Spirit is saying about someone, not just to look at how reliable or emotionally consistent or how good at presenting themselves they are. She reminds me of the importance of just loving people with the love of Jesus – no matter what they do or how far they run away. I reckon if she had been around in Jesus' day, Hana would have been one of the unexpected people in Luke's Gospel who teaches us something new about Jesus and His kingdom.

I would love to tell you about another friend of mine, Sophie. Sophie's story is very different from Hana's but just as amazing. The first time I met Sophie I was welcoming people to a café I was volunteering for at a Soul Survivor festival. I remember noticing she was unusually small and looked a bit fragile. I didn't have a clue then how incredibly tough she was! She asked me about our church as she was coming to Salford to study. I usually assume people won't like our church because it's a bit different, so I gave her a copy of my first book (which tells our story) and said, 'Have a read of this, and if you're still interested in coming when you've finished it, you will probably fit in well with us!'

I was very glad when Sophie turned up at LCC on a Sunday a few weeks later. I remember driving her home and telling her about all the other churches in the area, in case she might prefer one of them, but she kept coming back to us, so I figured she must be pretty cool, as well as a bit crazy. She would fit in well.

We had the privilege of getting to hear some of Sophie's story as the weeks unfolded. She was born early, weighing only 2lb 14oz, and spent the first month of her life in ICU. Very early on, her parents realised they had to put her life in God's hands.

At only six months old, Sophie was diagnosed with a rare genetic blood condition called Diamond-Blackfan anaemia. In Sophie's case, it meant that she didn't produce red or white blood cells properly, making her very vulnerable to infection. She had to have blood transfusions every three to six weeks. Much of Sophie's childhood was spent in Royal Manchester Children's Hospital. At age ten, her bone marrow failed completely and she had to have chemotherapy to kill the old bone marrow, and then new bone marrow given as a blood transfusion. This led to full liver failure, terrible skin reactions and internal bleeding.

At this point many people were rallied to pray, and suddenly the bleeding ceased. The doctors couldn't explain why it had stopped. One night, as Sophie was being held by her dad, she experienced the love of God for the first time as she suddenly realised her Father God was holding her too. Sophie was able to recover, return to school, get baptised and complete her GCSEs. One night at a Soul Survivor event she fully committed her life to Jesus and had an experience of being filled with His compassion.

This compassion grew in her heart. Sophie began to realise that God wanted to use her experiences to help others, and started looking for courses in child nursing. Thankfully for us, Sophie chose to study in Salford. Of course, I always assume that God wants everyone to move to Salford. During her three years of study, Sophie has battled through a global pandemic, the pressure of long shifts and essay deadlines, and another health scare when she had internal bleeding and was blue-lighted to hospital with a blood clot, and lost weeks of her training. Despite all of this, she persevered and made it through.

Sophie started her final placement at Royal Manchester Children's Hospital on the very day of the eleventh anniversary of her transplant in that very same hospital. On her final day of university, exactly three years since she arrived in Salford, she was offered a job in the same hospital where she had spent so much of her childhood. The child who almost died on a number of occasions will now be part of a team helping to save the lives of many other children.

Sophie says, 'Knowing that I will start my nursing career in the same hospital where I had my treatment is the most perfect full circle, and an incredible example of how God has turned the most painful and frightening times of my life into something brand new and beautiful – He has worked every part of my life for good. "And we know that in all things God works for the good of those who love him, who have been called according to his purpose" [Romans 8:28]. Now I can use my experience to make sure my patients get the best care, and my prayer is that every day I show God's love to those I meet, and that His love and compassion make me a better nurse.'

What a story! What a God, who turns lives around and brings us healing, so much so that even the most difficult times can actually be turned around and used for the good of others! No one would have thought that the tiny baby with the rare genetic condition would now be part of a team saving the lives of other babies and children. No one except God. No one would have thought that Gideon the coward would lead Israel to victory with a tiny army against a powerful enemy. No one but God. No one would have thought that the abused teenager in a gang would become Rev Hana, church planter and all-round legend. No one but God.

This is what God does. This is the God who said no to all of David's older brothers and yes to the forgotten shepherd boy, because God 'looks at the heart', not the outer appearance (1 Samuel 16:7). This is the God who sent His Son to an obscure village on the outskirts of the empire, and gave the news of His birth to poor night-shift workers (the shepherds) and to foreigners who practised a different religion (the Magi).

If you feel forgotten about or overlooked or not good enough or that you don't fit the mould, or you find yourself living or working in some obscure backwater, you are exactly the kind of person in exactly the kind of place that God is interested in. You are not forgotten. This is the God who goes to the edges, the deserts, the unstrategic places. I pray that God would open our eyes to see beyond the surface and to the heart. I pray that God would enable us to see the gifts and not just the issues. I pray that God would give us the patience and humility to slow down and listen, and then the courage and boldness to follow where Jesus leads.

Consider the story of Mephibosheth, who we read about in 2 Samuel 9. The son of King David's beloved friend Jonathan, he was disabled from a young age when he was dropped by his nurse (2 Samuel 4:4). Most of his family, including his father Jonathan and grandfather Saul, had been killed, and Mephibosheth found himself an outcast, living in a lonely outpost called Lo Debar, which literally means 'nowhere place' or 'nothing town'. A man with no family, no hope and living in nowhere, who described himself as a 'dead dog' (2 Samuel 9:8), receives an invite to the king's table. And not just for a one-off charitable meal. From that point on he would always eat at the table of the king, and all his land would be restored to him, in an attempt by King David to show the kindness of God.

This is what God does, and just like David in this moment of clarity, we are also called to search for and find the treasures in the nowhere towns, and invite them to the table of the king. We are also called to show the kindness of God to those who see themselves as 'dead dogs' and help them realise their worth and the honour that comes only from an encounter at the table of the king.

Chapter Five
The Miracle of Just Enough

I started this book with the story of how our church Sunday attendance shrank by about half a few years ago. Maybe not the most inspiring story to begin with, but I figured it was best to tell you the truth. One of the consequences of this was that after a few months, we realised we were running out of money. We were losing about £525 a month, which meant that by the summer we would have nothing left. Now, Esther and I have seen God provide for us in amazing ways over the years, so I knew about God's faithfulness in times like this. But everyone who was left in the church was already giving so much – of their time, their prayers and their money. We decided to have a gift day.

Two weeks before the gift day, I spoke to the whole church and asked them to prayerfully consider giving more regular financial support. I acknowledged that they were already going above and beyond, but I explained the situation that we were in and asked them to pray over the next two weeks. Then I found myself saying, 'I have seen God provide so many times over the years, and if we are still obeying all He has called us to do, He will provide for us again.' I remember sitting down and thinking, 'But *will* He do it this time?'

Two weeks later I counted up our pledges. Amazingly, our little group had pledged another £250 a month, meaning we were about halfway towards what we needed.

The following day I had a phone call from a couple from another part of the country who had happened to be visiting us a fortnight before. They asked how the gift day had gone, so I said we were about halfway towards what we needed. They replied by saying, 'Well, we felt that God had told us to start giving you £275 a month starting this month.'

I was gobsmacked. Exactly what we needed. Not more, not less, just what we had been praying for and wondering where on earth it would come from. And from a couple who just 'happened' to be visiting on that particular day, who then felt stirred to give us the exact amount that we needed. This is the goodness and faithfulness of God. We so needed to be reminded of that in those dark days. He is so kind to us.

I tell that story because so many of us have experienced similar things as we try to follow God's call to step out into the unknown. Before I look further into this, let's return to our telling of the Bible story. In the last chapter we looked at the period of the judges, that strange in-between time in the Bible story that follows the Exodus and precedes the glory days of David and Solomon. We have already mentioned how David was anointed by the prophet Samuel, despite being the least of his brothers and not even thought worthy of consideration to be king. Yet this humble shepherd boy would go on to be considered the greatest of Israel's kings, and a model of the future Messiah. His son and heir Solomon would continue this age of expansion and prosperity for the nation in his lifetime. Many of the biblical wisdom books are linked to these two kings and the flourishing of creativity during their reigns, and Solomon would go on to build the temple in Jerusalem.

However, after these glory years, the excesses of Solomon's reign (he had 700 wives and 300 concubines, and used forced labour to build the temple for the God who had freed His people from slavery – see 1 Kings 11:3; 2 Chronicles 2:1–2) led to division and war, with his sons fighting for power. Eventually this led to the break-up of the kingdom, with Israel (sometimes called Ephraim) in the north and Judah (with its capital Jerusalem) in the south. This disaster for the people of God ushered in an era of decline and apostasy. Most of the kings led the people away from God, with only occasional revivals under leaders like Josiah and Hezekiah. This got worse and worse until the northern kingdom fell to Assyria in 722BC and Judah eventually succumbed to the Babylonians in 586BC. Jerusalem and the temple were destroyed, and the people exiled to Babylon.

It was during these dark centuries (described in the books of Kings and Chronicles) that the great prophets arose. They tended to have three roles. Some spoke to the rulers and called them to do justly and treat the people with compassion and mercy. They also called the people back to God. And finally they pointed to the future – first to an imminent judgement for sin, but also to an eventual deliverer to come – a new covenant, forgiveness, restoration and a new anointed leader who would bring peace and freedom once again.

The first in the line of these great prophets is Elijah. I've got a lot of time for Elijah as he is a northerner. His story is epic, packed full of miracles, battles and amazing prophetic words. One of the fascinating episodes of his life is during a famine when God sends him to Zarephath to find food (1 Kings 17:7-16). God directs him to a widow at the town gate. He asks her for food and drink, and she confesses to him that she has run out of food and is about to prepare her final meal so that she and her son can eat it before they die. Elijah tells her not to be afraid, and then instructs her to make food for him as well as her family, and promises her that her flour and oil will not run out until rain returns to the land. Day after day she will return to the jar of flour and jug of oil, only to find there is just enough for that day.

Sam and Katy from The Groves Church call this 'the miracle of just enough'. I love that phrase. For Sam and Katy, it has summarised much of their experience of pioneering a new church in an estate in Chester. Whether financial provision or bringing the right people at the right time, God has always provided them with the miracle of just enough. Katy has struggled with chronic fatigue syndrome over the past few years and there have been many occasions when she has reached the end of a day feeling that she will have a crash the next day and not be able to do what is needed, but each time she has experienced God's provision of enough energy for that day.

Reflecting on this experience, they both talked about the deep learning that comes from this. From their charismatic tradition, the expectation would have been that the miracle would come all at once – an instant healing and everything is changed. But for them (and so many others), it has been just enough for that day. His 'mercies ... are new every morning' (Lamentations 3:22-23, NRSVA). We would prefer the big bang and the spectacular miracle, but in turning to God for the day-to-day miracles, we learn to rely on Him. We learn to not treat our relationship with God like an occasional visit to the doctor to get us sorted, but to utterly rely on Him for our daily bread.

There is a fragility in this kind of calling. My friend Robin is one of the leaders at Barton Community Church near Oxford. Their immersion in that 'end-of-the-line' estate over the past ten years has produced some deep learning and a wonderful church community that reflects the place where it is rooted. Robin says, 'It has felt like it's been held together by sellotape. But God has always provided enough sellotape.' The miracle of just enough.

This is like the manna in the desert. Store up more than you need for that day, and it goes rotten (Exodus 16:20). Take just enough, and then come back again tomorrow, the next day and every day. Life in the desert requires a total reliance on God's provision. It isn't easy, but it teaches us about the faithfulness of God. It is why when Jesus sent the disciples out He commanded them to take no supplies with them (Luke 10:4). God wants us to learn just how faithful He is when we follow His call. This is not the comfortable road to take. To be honest with you, it can be a bit annoying sometimes.

When my wife Esther and I spent a few years trusting God for our income, we were praying for £100 to pay a bill.

On the day we had to pay, £100 arrived in an envelope with a letter saying, 'I was going to send this two weeks ago but God told me to wait till today.' I was not too happy about this; it would have been a lot easier for my stress levels if it had come two weeks earlier! When we raised money to employ a new manager for our LifeCentre community hub, it was on the day that Beth started her job that exactly the right money came in to finance her first year in post. When I was a trustee with Soul Survivor, God always gave us enough for that year. We never had a huge surplus or a rich benefactor; it was always a daily walk with the Lord and a constant trust in Him. It was a miracle of just enough. We don't get ahead of ourselves; we simply trust in the One who has sent us.

There have been many times over the years with LCC when I have got really frustrated with God and said, 'If only we could have a few more families join us. If only we could have some rich person who gives us a solid income then we don't need to think about money for a while.' And every time God says, 'What is that in your hand'?' Remember that question to Moses? Every time, we are reminded, 'My grace is sufficient for you, for my power is made perfect in weakness' (2 Corinthians 12:9). But I don't want to be weak! It's easier to be self-sufficient. It feels more comfortable to be strong and secure.

Elijah knows what it is to be utterly reliant on God. When he meets the widow at Zarephath, he knows that nothing is too difficult for God, after experiencing God's miraculous provision at the Kerith Ravine (1 Kings 17:2-6). Each day, even though it looks like it's going to run out, there is enough.

I meet so many people who are pioneering new mission initiatives in marginalised places who have this feeling that the oil and flour is about to run out. So many people who have had wonderful miracles happen over the years, but they are facing a new lack and are needing to believe again, like we did as a church a few years ago when lots of people left and our money started to run out. I looked round and thought, 'How can this still happen? We are all so tired and weary and hurt. Is there a future for us as a church community? Who will do this role, who can replace that person?'

I remember some people in the church coming to me and saying, 'We are with you. We've got your back.' I remember others giving money, and many others praying for us. All of these small, seemingly isolated acts combine together to produce a clear *keep going, trust Me* message from God!

Elijah's story is also fascinating because of the extreme highs and lows. We have seen miracles and disasters in one day. We have had incredible financial provision followed by a phone call from a friend in deep despair. A stunning sense of God's presence in worship, then the news that someone is struggling in their marriage. And emotionally it can be the same. Feeling the love and support of your friends, then arriving home and wanting to pack it all in. Elijah goes from an awesome victory over the prophets of Baal to fleeing to the desert, crushed by depression and wanting to die. What does God do? He provides food for Elijah. Just enough food. Enough to set him on a journey through the desert to the mountain of God, where he would be revived and commissioned again by the divine whisper (1 Kings 19:1-13).

I remember having one of our best and most exciting church gatherings where it felt like we were seeing wonderful breakthroughs in people's lives, then walking home and slumping down on the sofa, and all I could hear in my mind was, 'You can't do this. It's all going to fall apart. You've not got what it takes. You're not good enough.' My energy was spent and it felt like I couldn't move, and I started to plan my exit strategies!

This kind of adrenaline crash is not rare, but I do think there is also a real spiritual battle that we are in, and the biggest lows can often come after the biggest highs. In those moments it is vital to have people we can call or text, who we know will pray for us straight away.

Another thing Elijah experiences, which I have found in my life and that of many other pioneers, is a deep and recurring sense of loneliness. Elijah says – twice – with deep sadness, 'I am the only one ... left' (1 Kings 18:22; 1 Kings 19:10). One of the most special moments in following Jesus to the margins is when you discover that you are not the only one left. God corrects Elijah and points out that there are 7,000 who are still faithful (1 Kings 19:18). He is not the only one.

Often when we are doing the hard graft of breaking new ground it can be a lonely experience. Over the years we have had a number of friends come alongside us to give us great advice, but often what we have found is that they are advising us on how we can become more like the church they are involved with, which doesn't really fit what we are doing. Not every model is the same. We need to become who God has called us to be. There can be pain involved when well-meaning friends try to help but it becomes clear that they don't quite 'get' what we are trying to do. That's when the loneliness kicks in. Like Elijah, you may be tempted to think, 'It's just me, I'm the only one left!' Does anyone understand?

One of the greatest joys for me over the last few years has been when people have emailed me from different parts of the country saying, 'We read your story and we were so relieved that other people are doing something similar! We thought it was just us!' Then I get the joy of meeting them and listening to their story, and friendships are born in those moments when we realise we are not alone. We tell a story and the other person nods knowingly, because they have been through it too, and the smile that they give us contains the pain and joy of years of living this out in their own lives. We are not the only one left.

Some of the people I have been telling you about in this book have done that for us here in Langworthy. They 'get it'. I am convinced that it is possible to live healthily in these situations of vulnerability and utter reliance on God. One of the keys to this is finding people who will accompany us on the journey. People who 'get it'. They might work closely with us, or they might live hundreds of miles away and we only see them a few times a year, but they are life-givers. We don't have to explain ourselves to them. They laugh in the middle of one of our stories because they know how it is going to end, because they've been there too and experienced the same painful/beautiful thing. They make us feel understood and known, and, perhaps most importantly, they make us feel *at home*.

If you are on a journey like Abraham and you have obeyed a call to leave behind your home comforts and go to a place God will show you, but you actually don't know where you are going, you can often experience a sense of homelessness: 'Where do I belong? I've left behind everything I know and don't fit in back there any more, but I've not yet reached my new destination, so what is home for me now?' Like the people of Israel in their tents trekking round the desert, they had left Egypt but not yet arrived at the Promised Land. Who were they? Would they ever reach their destination? They followed the cloud and the fire, constantly adapting, always ready to move, continually reliant on the daily manna (Exodus 13:20–22; 16).

It is interesting that under the rule of King David, the ark of the tabernacle, symbolising the presence of God, was kept in a tent. When it was in a tent, it was much more accessible than when the temple was eventually built. In that time even the Gentiles could come in to worship God, and there was constant singing and worship twenty-four hours a day, with singers and musicians prophesying and singing new songs to God (1 Chronicles 16). It was a time of great innovation and freedom. It was mobile, accessible, spontaneous and Spirit-filled.

Later, Amos would prophesy the restoration of David's tent (Amos 9:11-12), and the disciples would use that prophecy to support the inclusion of the Gentiles in Acts 15. Indeed, those words we just used would be a great summary of the earliest Church described by Luke in the book of Acts – mobile, accessible, spontaneous, Spirit-filled. It is significant that the prophecy was about restoring David's tent rather than Moses' tabernacle or Solomon's temple.

Where was 'home' for these mobile movements, whether in the Sinai desert in the days of Moses, the people in the days of David, or the pioneering missionaries of the earliest Church? As I said in chapter three, central to all of them is the presence of God – the hosting of His presence. The encounter with the Divine.

If I could have one thing in the whole world, something worth giving up everything else for, it would be God's presence. I know He is always with me, but there is something wonderful that happens when we pursue His tangible presence in our lives and our gatherings.

There have been moments in my life when God has been kind enough to bless me with a tangible sense of His presence. I remember sitting in a meeting at the Soul Survivor youth festival and suddenly sensing God, and it was so utterly wonderful that I didn't dare move because it felt so holy and beautiful and I didn't want it to ever stop. In that moment I desperately wanted to gather everyone I had ever met into that big draughty tent so they could share this with me. More than anywhere else it felt like *home*. I could have stayed there forever.

I remember sitting on St Cuthbert's Isle off the Holy Island of Lindisfarne and experiencing a peace that permeated every part of my body and soul, and praying longingly to God that I could keep it forever, hoping that it could be part of what home would mean for me.

There was another time a couple of years ago when I was on a retreat and visited Buckfast Abbey near Plymouth. We had just come through some of the toughest moments of our church struggles, and we were regrouping and asking God what was next. The retreat had been a fairly pleasant time but I hadn't really had any sense of what God was saying, except that it was a time for me to relax and be still. I wandered round the grounds and it was all very nice, but again, nothing unusual.

Just as I was about to leave, I decided to pop into the little chapel at the end of the abbey. I knelt down and closed my eyes. Immediately I heard God say to me, 'Do you want this?'

I wasn't sure what 'this' was, but figured that if God was offering it, I had better say yes, so I whispered, 'Yes, please!'

What happened next was a unique experience in my life so far. It was incredibly intense and as if God was filling me almost violently with His Spirit. I was aware of other people in the room and made every effort to not make any noise, but it was a battle. Every now and again I would whisper, 'Wowww,' under my breath as I tried to cope with the intensity of it all! God spoke to me incredibly clearly and quite forcefully in those moments.

When I opened my eyes it seemed like only a few minutes had gone by, but it was actually an hour and a half. I staggered out of the chapel and made my way home. And yet, in those ninety minutes, that is when I was truly home.

I knew I had to step out in faith again. I needed to write another book (this one!) and to put some time into gathering people together who were called to similar ministries to ours, to support each other and pray together. But it would take time and I would need to give up a day a week of my paid work to make it happen. Esther and I agreed that we would trust that God would provide for us as a family. When we had done this before it was just the two of us, but now we had three kids and it felt slightly more scary!

Soon after I got back, I happened to be in a meeting with a friend and someone I hadn't met before, discussing the future of an organisation that I had been a part of. We ended up talking together about what I was feeling God calling me to do and, completely out of the blue, they offered to support me financially for one day a week for a two-year period! Another amazing provision from God, totally unexpected. It was exactly the amount of money we needed. Not more, and not less. The miracle of just enough.

These are the moments I long for the most – not the provision stories (although they are so important), but the 'Presence' moments. When an hour and a half feels like five minutes. When 1,000 years is like a day (2 Peter 3:8). When I just want everyone I have ever met to come and share this moment with me! This is the heart of it all for me. This is home when we feel homeless.

This is what the world needs more than anything. It is what everyone longs for even if they can't put it into words. Just before the first national lockdown (owing to the coronavirus pandemic), Beth and I went out onto Salford Precinct with two of our vicar friends. It was Ash Wednesday and we had decided it would be a good idea to see if the shoppers of Salford would like us to smear some ashes on their foreheads in the shape of a cross and to pray a prayer reminding them that they were one day going to die.

The two vicars were wearing their full-length black cassocks and brought the ashes and written prayers. Beth and I came in jeans and warm coats and nervous smiles, and we split into twos. We put it into a hashtag to make it sound cooler – #ashestogo – but the fact was that we were about to try to interrupt people's shopping trips to tell them they were going to die and then offer to make their foreheads dirty. That didn't sound cool.

The next two hours were amazing.

During those two hours we prayed with at least forty different people, and at least half of them wanted the ashes. Everyone was incredibly grateful for our prayers. Lots of them cried as we prayed. A few said, 'You've made my day,' and asked when and where our churches met. While one of the two read out the Ash Wednesday prayer, the other listened for the whisper of the Spirit and shared spontaneous prayers and words we felt that God was giving us for each person.

We experienced the coming of the beautiful presence of God time and time again that morning. We were like a mobile tent hosting the presence of God, on the path between the supermarket and the charity shop. It was the same Spirit who filled me in Buckfast Abbey and in a big tent at Soul Survivor. The same Spirit who spoke to Elijah in the 'gentle whisper' (1 Kings 19:12) was present with us next to the trolleys and the guy smoking weed. We even prayed for someone who told us he was John the Baptist! As we prayed for him we sensed the same presence that descended like a dove onto Jesus when He was baptised by the actual John the Baptist (Matthew 3:16).

I could see in people's eyes that morning as they began to cry, a feeling of coming home. Often our prayers would lead them to start sharing something about their childhood, or an experience of God they'd had when they were younger. There is something in all of us that longs for home, like the prodigal son in Luke 15 longing for the embrace of his father. We need to get out there again and again and offer this to people. We cannot keep it for ourselves. In streets, workplaces, homes, let us pray together that ancient prayer of the Church: 'Come, Holy Spirit.' Come into our lives and bring all the beauty of God. Reassure us, provoke us, send us out to spread this love to others.

Come, Holy Spirit. We are hungry for You. We long for more people to share the wonder of coming home to Your presence. We need You to meet us when we slump into a chair and hear the lies of the enemy telling us we can't do this any more. We need to know Your presence in the thin places[11] like Holy Island and Buckfast Abbey, but also in our day-to-day conversations, in head teachers' offices, outside charity shops, and in the presence of those who nod and smile at our stories and remind us that we are not alone.

Come, Holy Spirit.

---

[11] So called because the 'veil' between heaven and earth seems to be particularly thin.

Chapter Six
Exile and Return

One thing I have noticed when talking to people whom God has called to the *tohu* and *bohu* ministries is, if you ask them whether God gave them some prophetic scriptures about their hopes and dreams for their estate, the verses are nearly always from the book of Isaiah. The Eden Movement,[12] an incarnational mission organisation that started in Manchester, has the wonderful words of Isaiah 35 as foundational to its vision: 'Water will gush forth in the wilderness and streams in the desert' (Isaiah 35:6). Sam and Katy in Chester hold on to 41:18: 'I will make rivers flow on barren heights, and springs within the valleys. I will turn the desert into pools of water, and the parched ground into springs.' My friends Ben and Amy, planting churches in estates around Bolton, emphasise 61:4: 'They will rebuild the ancient ruins and restore the places long devastated.'

Our church in Langworthy is no exception to this! We have always come back to the words of Isaiah 60:1, 18:

> Arise, shine, for your light has come,
> and the glory of the LORD rises upon you …

---

[12] See message.org.uk/eden (accessed 14th February 2022).

> No longer will violence be heard in your land …
> you will call your walls Salvation and your gates
> Praise.

We also have prayed for the vision of chapter 54 to come
to pass:

> Afflicted city, lashed by storms and not
> comforted,
> I will rebuild you …
> All your children will be taught by the LORD,
> and great will be their peace …
> you will have nothing to fear.
> (Isaiah 54:11-14)

It has been wonderful over the years to watch as an estate
once ruled by fear and violence has changed so much, and
our work with the schools means that thousands of
children over the past two decades have been taught about
the Lord.

One fascinating verse I noticed recently was Isaiah
49:17. The NRSVA translates it as, 'Your builders outdo
your destroyers, and those who laid you waste go away
from you.' There is some debate as to whether 'builders'
should be translated as 'sons', but this idea of builders
outdoing destroyers really interested me. It feels like
something we have seen in our estate over the years, and
in the lives of individuals too. When we first moved in
there were many destroyers, who really ruled the area.
There was an atmosphere of fear and intimidation that we
could literally feel in the air as we walked around the
streets. But there came a stage where people who wanted
to build something – actually, to rebuild – gained more

confidence, and began to step out and provide hope to others who also wanted to rebuild.

The community that had been scared into their houses began to emerge again. One lady led an amazing project putting flowers around the estate, eventually winning awards from Britain in Bloom. Shopkeepers were part of a project where the ugly shutters on their windows were removed and relocated to the inside, so the shops looked more welcoming again, more confident. The builders began to outdo the destroyers. And many of the destroyers just seemed, as the verse says, to go away.

Likewise, many people have destructive influences in their lives that don't always disappear, but when they meet Jesus and join a church, there can be an effect by which the builders outdo the destroyers, and they experience healing and growth.

Of course, when these prophecies were originally given, the prophets did not have in mind the Langworthy estate of the early twenty-first century. They are not automatic promises from God that we can just pick off a page and put on our fridges as a guarantee of the future of our communities. However, God can use these ancient words to encourage anyone in any generation in history, including our own.

I think it is fascinating that the most common book that inspires these kinds of transformational visions is Isaiah. The prophecies in the book speak into a particular historical context. Let's take a minute to explore that context.

The prophecies in Isaiah are greatly influenced by a series of events that we now know as the Exile. As we mentioned earlier, the people of the northern kingdom were exiled in 722BC, and this happened during the fifty-year ministry of the prophet, which is outlined in chapters 1–39, a section sometimes known as First Isaiah. From chapter 40 onwards, there is a significant change in tone and focus, and it is as if Isaiah is speaking from the future, during the time of the southern exile in 586BC. Then later in the book, the writer seems to be addressing the exiles as they return to the land, from 536BC.

We have two choices in how to read this. Either it is written by one person to whom God gives supernatural foresight to know exactly what would happen in the southern exile, and even the name of the Persian King Cyrus. Alternatively (as most scholars believe), it is written by two or even three people, each speaking in the line of Isaiah but to different time periods. It seems unlikely to me that the prophet in chapters 40–55 would write directly to the exiles in Babylon, when the exile was yet to happen, so my guess is that there are two or three writers.

What I find fascinating here is that this great poetry, these soaring prophecies that continue to encourage and inspire church planters and pioneers in 'forgotten' estates thousands of years later and hundreds of miles away, were written in times of great upheaval and national trauma. They address the people in their times of greatest disaster – the loss of the sovereignty of both parts of the divided kingdom – but worst of all, the destruction of the temple and the ending of the royal line of King David, a line of succession that God had promised would never end (2 Samuel 7:16).

There is a theme of being uprooted in the Bible – in the very beginning when Adam and Eve were expelled from the garden, or when Abram was called to leave behind everything he knew, but this latest event was unimaginable. All the promises of God seemed to be undone. In the ancient world, the natural conclusion would have been that the Babylonian god had defeated the God of Israel and that the people would most likely have just integrated into their new setting and left behind their God who had seemingly abandoned them, or at least not been strong enough to protect them.

The fascinating thing that happens to the people of Israel is that their faith is actually made stronger instead. A look through the poems of Lamentations shows us the trauma and anguish of the people:

> My eyes fail from weeping,
> I am in torment within;
> my heart is poured out on the ground
> because my people are destroyed.
> (Lamentations 2:11)

And yet, even in this darkest night, the poet finds some hope:

> Because of the LORD's great love we are not consumed,
> for his compassions never fail.
> They are new every morning;
> great is your faithfulness.
> (Lamentations 3:22-23)

The verses of greatest hope and inspiration are often written in times of greatest disaster and trauma. The exiles of 722BC and 586BC were cataclysmic, and yet they ultimately led to renewal and repentance. Psalms of lament were written about singing 'the songs of the LORD' 'by the rivers of Babylon' (Psalm 137:4, 1). But the great prophets spoke words of hope:

> For a brief moment I abandoned you,
> but with deep compassion I will bring you back.
> In a surge of anger
> I hid my face from you for a moment,
> but with everlasting kindness
> I will have compassion on you.
> (Isaiah 54:7-8)

The exiles had to learn to adapt to a situation where their religion was a tiny minority. They were misunderstood and marginalised. They were seen as foolish and weak, and were powerless in a country that was not their own. Another great prophet of the exile, Jeremiah, advised them to:

> Build houses and settle down; plant gardens and eat what they produce. Marry and have sons and daughters … seek the peace and prosperity of the city to which I have carried you into exile. Pray to the LORD for it, because if it prospers, you too will prosper.
> (Jeremiah 29:5-7)

Look at the situation of the exiles here and compare it to the Church today. There are obviously huge differences, but there are some useful links. The Church is an increasingly small minority that is misunderstood and marginalised. In the Western world, the Christendom structures that gave the Church power and influence are crumbling and it is increasingly seen as irrelevant. Annual statistics show Church attendance declining rapidly in most parts of the UK and Europe.[13] There is widespread panic and money is being thrown at all kinds of new initiatives to try to stop the rot.

One of the reasons I think it is important that churches in the marginalised communities tell their stories is that we have been in this kind of situation for a long time! Whether in inner-city estates or rural outposts, we have known what it is like to feel small, vulnerable and powerless for a long time. And as the whole Church catches up with those on the margins, it needs to hear our stories and benefit from our learning.

One of the keys in this passage from Jeremiah is this stunning phrase:

> I have carried you into exile.
> (Jeremiah 29:7)

I decided it was important enough to put it on one line. It wasn't the weakness of God that led to the Exile. God hadn't been defeated by the gods of Assyria and Babylon. God had *carried* them into exile. If we are to be attentive to what God is doing in our generation, to the 'exile' we find ourselves in, we don't need to be scrambling around for the latest course or leadership conference or style of church planting. We need to repent. As Stefan Paas says in his brilliant book *Pilgrims and Priests*, as a Church we need

---

[13] For UK statistics, see faithsurvey.co.uk/uk-christianity.html (accessed 6th January 2022).

to 'learn what it means to be weak and foolish'.[14] We need to identify why God has led us here, and how He wants us to serve Him in this generation.

We need to embrace powerlessness. Surely this is what Paul is talking about in Philippians 2 when he tells us to have the same mind as Jesus, who 'made himself nothing' (v7) and gave His life for others. Paul was also living in a land ruled by a mighty and oppressive empire, and travelled around to many places where Christianity seemed a bizarre and foreign idea.

In its origins, the Christian faith was a faith of the oppressed and marginalised. Read Luke's Gospel to see how Jesus always ate with the sinners and rejects, as we mentioned earlier. As the faith spread throughout the world in the first three centuries, the Christians had to meet in homes and often in secret. There were no magnificent buildings or links with governments, and their teaching and practices were dismissed as an odd superstition or even as a dangerous and subversive rebellion.

Thomas and Claudia in Edinburgh talk about 'taking on powerlessness' in their calling to Stenhouse. There is a temptation in mission to see the huge needs and take on a saviour complex, where we bring skills and resources to sort people's lives out, bringing our answers to questions that may have not been asked.

Everyone I spoke to when writing this book testified to this same experience, of coming in with answers and skills, and realising they had to put them to one side in order to first listen and learn. Ben and Amy in Bolton told

---

[14] Stefan Paas, *Pilgrims and Priests* (London: SCM Press, 2019), p40.

me that they went into the estate with their 'toolkit' oɪ things they knew worked in similar contexts, ready to hit the ground running. They quickly realised that God wanted them to down tools and spend months in a posture of prayerful listening – listening to the Spirit and to the community. It was only then that they were able to respond to God in creating something contextual for that particular place.

Sam and Katy talk about a similar experience: 'We had all our ducks lined up, things that we know work well in terms of reaching and discipling people. Then God knocked all our ducks down.' They describe a painful process of realising that 'no strategy in the world can build the Church; only Jesus can', redefining what success looks like, learning to walk at the pace of Jesus and coping with disappointment. The exiles in Babylon found themselves having to redefine what their faith looked like. They could no longer go to the temple to offer sacrifices, and their faith was a confusing oddity to those around them.

And yet... And yet this traumatic period saw a refining of their faith in God. The story of the expulsion from the Garden of Eden was retold and written down, as the people reached back to their founding stories to rediscover their identity. There was a purifying effect, and the 'holy stump' (see Isaiah 6:13) that had been pruned by the Gardener began to grow again.

If the Church is under the judgement of God today, we need to humbly accept the purifying effects of our own exile. We need to humble ourselves and learn to trust completely in God when our resources are rapidly diminishing and we continue to decline in numbers. We have a new opportunity to be reminded again of the utter

ess of God in the most difficult times. We can be
to this in a rapidly changing world that has been
sed by the pandemic, racism and violence.

As our own faith and practice, until very recently assumed to be logical and obvious, becomes increasingly sidelined, perhaps we can learn from Henri Nouwen's words a generation ago: 'The Christian leader of the future is called to be completely irrelevant and stand in this world with nothing to offer but his or her own vulnerable self.'[15] In a Church often obsessed with relevance, it is surely more powerful to offer ourselves in vulnerability. Offering our stories and experiences, our time and hospitality. Not trying to coerce or control but to follow the gentle leading of the Spirit.

One book that shaped me more than most was *The Pastor*, the autobiography of Eugene Peterson. In it he makes this statement: 'My work is not to fix people. It is to lead people in the worship of God and to lead them in living a holy life.'[16] This is such an important antidote to our constant need to save people, or, more accurately, to be the saviours of people. Jesus is the Saviour. We don't need to do His job for Him. We need to be saved.

It is in times of exile that we need to hear the prophets. Where are the Isaiahs of today, the poets calling us back to God, giving us hope and boldly calling out the sin and injustice of our day? Where are the modern Jeremiahs, who weep with the deep compassion of God over the brokenness of our age, and yet remind us of God's

---

[15] Henri Nouwen, *In The Name of Jesus* (London: DLT, 1989), p17.
[16] Eugene H Peterson, *The Pastor* (New York: HarperCollins, 2011), p137.

faithfulness and teach us how to live in exile? Or how about Ezekiel, another prophet of the Exile, who gives us a glimpse of heaven, who understands the deep trauma and anger of a generation, and whose visions give us hope that in a valley of dry bones, new life can come (Ezekiel 37)? We need to pray for the poet-prophets to rise up, not to act like fortune tellers but to draw our hearts back to the Father, to awaken the ancient dream of Eden, to call the bones to live again.

At the conclusion of the Old Testament narrative, the Exile comes to an end when God anoints a pagan king, Cyrus of Persia, to do His will and send the exiles back to the land in 536BC after a fifty-year exile. We read the stories of the return to the land in the books of Ezra and Nehemiah, and in the words of the prophets Haggai, Zechariah and Malachi. They provide some hope for the future – while the temple is being rebuilt, Haggai prophesies a greater glory than that of the first temple (Haggai 2:9), and Malachi foresees the Lord returning to the temple after being heralded by a messenger (Malachi 3:1).

Despite the great hopes of restoration for Jerusalem, and the people now being back in the land, there is still a longing for deliverance. They are ruled over by a succession of empires – the Persians, then the Greeks and eventually the Romans. They are left to wrestle with their longing to see the kingdom of God come 'on earth as it is in heaven'. The words of the prophets tantalise and frustrate them, and yet give them hope.

Expectations eventually developed of a deliver who would come to save them, an anointed one, or 'Messiah'. Would it be a great hero like Moses who would lead a new exodus (Deuteronomy 18:18) and lead to a new covenant as prophesied by Jeremiah (Jeremiah 31:31)? Or the mysterious Servant described by Isaiah during the Exile, who would somehow take the sin of the world upon Himself, and by His wounds they would be healed (Isaiah 53:5)? Would God Himself somehow come as their Good Shepherd, as Ezekiel suggests, to give them a heart of flesh and sprinkle clean water on them and restore them again (Ezekiel 34; Ezekiel 36:25-26)? What about the ruler spoken of by Micah who would emerge from Bethlehem and 'whose origins are … from ancient times' (Micah 5:2)? Or Zechariah's king who will come bringing salvation, 'lowly and riding on a donkey' (Zechariah 9:9)? Who was the divine human described by the prophet Daniel who enters the throne room of God and is given 'authority, glory and sovereign power' and 'all nations and peoples of every language worshipped him' (Daniel 7:13-14)? Would a king come again to restore the line of David, which God had said would never end (2 Samuel 7:12-13)?

These different images would provide plenty of food for thought over the centuries, and if you know the New Testament, they would be drawn upon by the early Christians as they tried to process what had happened in the life, death and resurrection of Jesus.

What I want to do here is end with that sense of longing. In the same way as the psalmist asked, 'How long, LORD?' (Psalm 13:1), I want to express that longing for home. A longing for Jesus and His wonderful presence. Jesus' disciples would use the Aramaic term *Marana tha*, meaning, 'Come, Lord' (1 Corinthians 16:22; see also Revelation 22:20).

Just as we relate to the exiles, we also pray with those who returned and found that it was not as they had hoped. We pray with the disappointed ones, the disillusioned and the frustrated. We pray with those who were oppressed for their whole lives. We cry out together: '*Marana tha*. Come, Lord Jesus.'

Chapter Seven
Hearing the Gospel

There is a long history of weird prophets in the Bible. Isaiah walked around 'stripped and barefoot' for three years (Isaiah 20). Imagine if he was part of your church! That would have been awkward on a Sunday morning. Ezekiel started off his ministry by eating a scroll (Ezekiel 3:3). He also cooked his food on dung (Ezekiel 4:12) and lay on one side for 390 days! (Ezekiel 4:4-5). And as for some of his visions…

At the end of this long line of prophetic strangeness comes John. He is very much in the mould of the Old Testament prophets, but he appears in the New Testament. He is living in the desert, wearing a hair shirt and enjoying an interesting diet of locusts and honey. He is clearly quite a character! The great line of prophets starting with Elijah leads us to John, who we are told comes 'in the spirit … of Elijah' (Luke 1:17). The New Testament writers link him to the voice crying 'in the wilderness, "Prepare the way for the Lord"' (Matthew 3:3), and to the messenger prophesied by Isaiah and Malachi who will prepare the way of the Lord (Isaiah 40:3; Malachi 3:1; Mark 1:2).

Just like the great prophets over all those centuries before him, John also speaks to the rulers to rebuke them – which is why he eventually gets his head cut off. He calls the people to return to God, standing in a river in the desert where the people first entered the Promised Land. In that river of beginnings, he calls the people to a new beginning. And he also points to the future – both to imminent judgement that is to come and to the coming Messiah.

I sometimes like to imagine all those other prophets from across the centuries who also pointed to the future Saviour feeling perhaps a bit jealous as John does so. When he says, 'Look, the Lamb of God, who takes away the sin of the world' (John 1:29), the Lamb of God who takes away the sin of the world is not many centuries away, but is walking by the river to meet him! This is the incredible privilege that John has. The hope of all the ages, the fulfilment of all the longings of the oppressed and enslaved, the new deliverer, God's own Son – is actually here. Not only that, He is in a queue to be baptised.

Imagine this scene. Jesus just joins the queue of sinners. Remember Isaiah's prophecy, He 'was numbered with the transgressors' (Isaiah 53:12)? Count those in the queue to be baptised, maybe forty of them; Jesus could be number eighteen. He is counted among them. John hesitates to baptise Him because he knows who this is – he is not even worthy to untie Jesus' shoelaces, let alone baptise Him! But Jesus insists, and He goes under that water on behalf of all of us. This immersion is an anticipation of His death, which will be sooner than anyone expects at this time. And when He emerges from the water we get this wonderful glimpse of the Trinity – the Son representing us in our sin, the Father speaking, 'This is my Son, whom I love; with him I am well pleased,' and the Spirit descending on him like a dove (Matthew 3:16-17).

John now makes way for Jesus, and this world-changing three-year ministry begins. It begins in a river, in the wilderness. Remember Isaiah? God is doing a new thing, there is water 'in the wilderness' and there are 'streams in the wasteland' (Isaiah 43:20). Once again, breakthrough comes in the desert. Away from the bright lights of the big city, away from the glare of publicity. And what does Jesus do next? He is led into the desert where He spends forty days being 'tempted by the devil' (Luke 4), one day representing each year that His people wandered around the desert after the Exodus.

The people of Israel moaned about bread in their desert wanderings (Numbers 11:4-6). Jesus, fasting from food for forty days, is tempted to miraculously produce bread for himself to eat. He chooses to continue His fast, resisting also the other temptations of power and fame, and He emerges in the power of the Spirit. He went into the wilderness 'full of the Holy Spirit' and emerges from this time of prayer and fasting 'in the power of the Spirit' (Luke 4:1, 14).

One thing we have found as a church is that times of prayer with fasting have often led to deeper experiences of the power of God in our lives. The desert-like experience of fasting, of denying ourselves some of the basics of life in order to devote ourselves to prayer, sharpens the mind and makes us more attentive to the work of the Spirit.

Recently we started our year with a month of corporate fasting as a church. We would fast from all food for one day per week, and restrict our eating at other times to remind us to pray. I launched this season of prayer by reminding the church of Jesus' forty days and how He emerged in the power of the Spirit.

On the first day of corporate fasting, I had a call from one of our church members. Her pregnant daughter had been rushed into hospital with serious bleeding. The doctors had told her it was almost certainly a miscarriage. The mother asking for prayer reminded me of what we had said about God's power and asked me to call the church to prayer. I felt nervous. Had I hyped this up too much? Should I try to manage her expectations?

The next day we had a call to say that the bleeding had stopped and a scan had shown that the baby was absolutely fine. The doctors were stunned, and one actually said, 'It's like a miracle.' Obviously we agreed!

These times of fasting are really hard, and often people give up. Jesus must have been seriously tempted to turn that stone into bread. During one season of fasting, one church member couldn't cope any more and ordered a triple steak sandwich!

But the reality that we have seen is that when we follow the lead of the Spirit into the wilderness, both in a physical sense and in fasting and prayer, we often see remarkable breakthroughs in the midst of much difficulty and hardship.

In this chapter I want to look at some aspects of Jesus' life, and then in the next chapter to look in more depth at His teaching. One interesting study is to read the reactions that different people have to Jesus and His gospel. Earlier I shared this quote from Vincent Donovan:

> When the gospel reaches a people where they
> are, their response to that gospel is the church in
> a new place, and the song they will sing is that
> new, unsung song, that unwritten melody that
> haunts all of us.[17]

Former Archbishop of Canterbury Rowan Williams says something along the same lines:

> It is sound theology to say that there are things
> we shall never know about Jesus Christ and the
> written Word unless we hear and see what they
> do in ever-new contexts. Mission is not only the
> carrying of good news; it is the willingness to
> hear the good news as the Word goes abroad and
> is embedded in culture after culture.[18]

The stories in the Gospels and Acts are a series of events where the gospel of Jesus is heard again and again in 'ever-new contexts'. It is not just well-trained evangelists and leaders who can communicate it. We need to listen to the songs and sayings that emerge as we share God's Big Story with those who have never heard it before. In doing so, we will learn new things about the Bible and about Jesus, if only we are willing to listen.

Here is one example of how I heard the gospel in a fresh way, when I was reminded of the cost of discipleship. A friend of mine who had come to faith through our church came to me in a quite angry state. He had been helping at

---

[17] Donovan, *Christianity Rediscovered*, pxiv.
[18] Andrew Walls and Cathy Ross, *Mission in the 21st Century* (New York: Orbis, 2008), Foreword, pxi.

an event where some of the non-church young people we were working with had been visited by a team of students from an evangelistic training course. A couple of them shared their stories with the young people, and then did a short preach, which was along the lines of, 'Jesus said He came to give us life to the max – if you say this prayer your life will be changed forever. Your life will be so much better, you will go from darkness to light, you will be able to live the best life you can imagine.'

He was fuming because this was not his experience of the effects of the gospel and of following Jesus. 'I would say that your life gets *harder* when you become a Christian. Yes, you experience God's love and have a church family that love you no matter what, but that is only part of the story. They need to tell those kids the whole truth. Things get more complicated and you have to choose to live a more difficult way of life; you can't just do whatever you want any more.'

I was hearing the gospel again in a new context. He was teaching me that while Jesus did talk about living life to the full, as the students had rightly said (John 10:10), Jesus also said, 'Whoever wants to be my disciple must deny themselves and take up their cross daily and follow me' (Luke 9:23). This is why we need to listen deeply, because people's responses to the gospel can teach us so much. This call will cost us our whole lives. It is not just another string to our bow, or a self-improvement programme, or a new mindfulness class that happens on a Sunday morning.

Jesus once asked what people said about Him. Peter mentioned Elijah and John the Baptist, but then Jesus heard the gospel coming to Him through Peter's own lips:

'You are the Messiah, the Son of the living God' (Matthew 16:16). Peter also said, 'You have the words of eternal life. We have come to believe and to know that you are the Holy One of God' (John 6:68-69). Jesus hears it through Thomas' words when he sees Him risen from the dead: 'My Lord and my God' (John 20:28). Paul's experience is as though 'scales fell from [his] eyes' (Acts 9:18). Mary sums up the heart of the message of the earliest disciples when she simply says, 'I have seen the Lord' (John 20:18). A man who was born blind sums up his experience with the phrase, 'One thing I do know. I was blind but now I see' (John 9:25).

Through these people and so many more, the gospel is sung and said in new ways. It reminds me of a friend who explained her experience of meeting Jesus as 'like going from black and white to colour'. Claudia and Thomas in Stenhouse describe a fascinating process by which they were experiencing some deconstructing in their own theological thought, but hearing the gospel back from those they were reaching. One woman described the huge changes in her life after coming to faith by saying to them, 'I just know I am known by Jesus.'

It is fascinating and hugely important for us to listen to the gospel through the words of those experiencing it for the first time, because it can help us to communicate it more relevantly to others in similar circumstances, to expand our gospel vocabulary. Amy and Ben in Bolton had a number of these experiences. One person said that they were just surviving before they met Jesus, but now were really living. Another person felt like they had lived a few lifetimes in the two years since they had come to faith, compared to all the years before they knew Jesus –

not a minute of those two years was wasted. A third person told them that he saw the cross as a great leveller that enabled them to belong to a community of all backgrounds, abilities and classes, as all need a Saviour. What a great summary!

It is a great exercise to write these things down. The comments people make before they are socialised into your group's way of expressing faith are so important, and incorporating them into your language of faith can help to keep you accessible and avoid too much jargon.

It is also amazing to hear people pray out loud for the first time. It's a bit like when a child speaks for the first time – stumbling, unsure, but raw and authentic and utterly magical. I always feel like crying when I hear people's first prayers! Again, it is interesting to hear how people express their prayers in those early days, as we can learn a lot from them before they get into Christian clichés!

Earlier I quoted Vincent Donovan talking about a new song emerging as the gospel reaches new people and places. Bede tells the story of a seventh-century herdsman called Caedmon. He had little learning and no ability to sing, so whenever there was a feast, and the tradition demanded that each person take their turn to take the harp and sing, he would excuse himself. On one of these occasions, Caedmon sneaked away from the feast and started his nightshift in the field, looking after the animals. He fell asleep, and in his dream a man appeared to him and said 'Caedmon, sing me a song.' Caedmon made his excuses that he couldn't sing, but the man persisted, telling him to sing about 'the creation of all things'. [19] Caedmon opened his mouth and immediately began to sing words he had never heard before, in praise of the creator God. When he woke up he was able to remember the song, and went to see the great Abbess Hild who was in charge of the mixed monastery of Whitby. She was amazed by his ability to sing the gospel in the language of the people, and persuaded him to join the monastic community and devote his life to composing songs and poems that told the gospel in a language accessible to all.

There is something amazing and profound about the songs that emerge as people and communities encounter Jesus in their own setting. I remember taking our youth group to a Christian event in the 1990s. The meeting had gone on for a *long* time. Longer than any meeting should ever last for, even if a good meeting. Thankfully they had booked a well-known preacher to speak, who was a brilliant communicator, so I was confident that although he was starting his talk long after the meeting should have ended, he could save the day. He was very good. And *very* long. It was like a whole other meeting. Towards the end of the talk, the organisers even started playing music in the background as if to encourage him to finish preaching! Then it was over, and I breathed a sigh of relief as we prepared to leave to get some chips and hot sugary doughnuts, like you do after youth meetings.

We were premature. The hosts thanked the preacher, but then introduced *another* section of the meeting! Matt Redman, the well-known worship leader, was going to

---

[19] Bede, *A History of the English Church and People* (Middlesex: Penguin Books Ltd, 1955), p246.

lead us in a song. We got our coats on so we were ready to leave as soon as he was done. He started to sing a new song he had just written, all about worship being about Jesus rather than ourselves. After the first verse and chorus, the whole atmosphere in the room had changed. The restive, irritable teenage crowd were caught up in worship. There was a sense that the place where we were all gathered had suddenly become holy ground. I looked along the row of our own youth group. Two of the young people were crying. Another three were on their knees, in the presence of a holy God. Two more were praying for each other. I was overcome by this sense of wonder and God's presence, and just excited to sing words that expressed things that I had felt deeply but hadn't been able to articulate until that moment. We would have been happy for that meeting to go on for much longer if we could have experienced that sense of the presence of God.

It was only later that we heard the story behind the song – 'The Heart of Worship' – a song that would go all over the world and be sung by millions of people. Matt's church, Soul Survivor Watford, had been going through a time where people had become too focused on whether they enjoyed the times of worship in the church. Mike Pilavachi, the leader of the church, realised they had strayed away from what worship was all about, and decided to make the radical decision, for a time, to stop having a worship band to lead songs. Worship is not about what we can get but what we can give. So each person was invited to bring their worship each Sunday, whether a prayer or a reading, some kind of offering. They went through a long period where there were no musicians on a stage to play the songs they wanted to sing. And it was towards the end of this period, as they began to relearn what worship was all about, that Matt wrote this song, about what happens when we bring ourselves to Jesus without the music, reminding ourselves that worship is not about what we can *get*, but it is all about one person – Jesus Christ.

This is what happens when a group of people relearn the gospel again together. When we strip away the lights and sound and make space to hear God and bring all we are to God. It is no wonder to me that this song had that effect on so many people, including my own youth group, in that seemingly endless meeting. To use the words of Donovan again, that song put into words and a tune, 'that unwritten melody that haunts all of us'.[20] The song emerged in a time when all the familiar aspects of church had been taken away. You could call it a desert place – a place where someone noticed a bush that was on fire but not burning up, and realised they were on holy ground. Then the song somehow brought that sense of holy ground to a bored and restless group of teenagers. This is what God does.

When we started to really feel God calling us to pray for Langworthy, a couple of years before we actually moved into the estate, we used to spend a lot of time in prayer and intercession. Lots of our prayers were focused around Isaiah 60, especially the first few lines:

> Arise, shine, for your light has come,
> and the glory of the LORD rises upon you.
> See, darkness covers the earth

---

[20] Donovan, *Christianity Rediscovered*, pxiv.

and thick darkness is over the peoples,
but the LORD rises upon you
and his glory appears over you.
(Isaiah 60:1-2)

The estate in those days was seen as a very dark place. Very high crime rates, gangs running riot, people leaving the area to such an extent that you could buy a two-bedroom house for less than £1,000! We felt a stirring from God to sing those words – originally written for Jerusalem many centuries ago – over our estate and over our city. As we stretched our hands out towards the estate, my friend James led us in the refrain and we sensed God's presence with us in a wonderful way.

I remember saying to James afterwards, 'You should turn that into a song' – and he did. A couple of years later we led thousands of young people gathered in the Manchester Arena for the Soul Survivor: The Message 2000 event with those words, which had come together in a little prayer meeting with ten people.

This is often what happens in Christian ministry. We find treasures in the dark places, we find streams in the desert (see Isaiah 45:3, NRSVA; 43:20), we see burning bushes in the wilderness, and these things often can have an effect that far outstrips what we imagine to be possible. When Caedmon opened his mouth and began to sing, he didn't have a clue what it would lead to, but he stepped out in faith and obedience and his life was transformed, and many people heard the gospel through his words and melodies.

This obedience was a key part of Jesus' ministry. He said, 'The Son can do nothing by himself; he can do only what he sees his Father doing, because whatever the Father does the Son also does' (John 5:19). Jesus models for His followers a life of noticing what God is doing, and joining in with that. He doesn't centre his ministry strategically on reaching the most people, or the important/influential ones, or impressing people with his miracle-working abilities. He is 'led by the Spirit into the wilderness' (Matthew 4:1). He wanders around the little villages of Galilee, being stopped by needy people, visiting them in their homes, healing those who are ill, casting out demons. When the crowds want to make Him King He escapes into obscurity again (John 6:15).

One significant aspect of Jesus' ministry is His willingness to say what He needs to say, no matter what the cost. He is not in it for the acclaim. There is a pivotal moment in John 6 where, after healing many people, a huge crowd gathers around Him and He feeds all of them miraculously. That night He walks on the water and the next day, as news of this emerges, the crowd track Him down again to ask Him questions. These are key moments when Jesus could impress them further and gain an even larger following in order to communicate His message. But instead He says deliberately controversial things to them to provoke a response, such as, 'I am the bread that came down from heaven' (John 6:41). Then He starts telling them they need to eat His flesh and drink His blood (John 6:53)! Let's be honest, that might be quite off-putting.

This has such an effect that not only do the crowds leave Him and stop following Him, but many who had been called His disciples also turn their backs and stop following Him. This is the moment when Jesus turns to the Twelve, His closest friends, and says the words, 'You do not want to leave too, do you?' (John 6:67). How do you read Jesus' question here? I wonder if there might be a real sadness in His voice. Jesus has said what He knows needed to be said, but He also knows it is a hard thing for His followers to hear. Almost all of them have walked away. Simon Peter assures Jesus that the Twelve are still with Him, but Jesus must feel sadness at seeing many others, who had been close enough to Him to be called His disciples, turning their backs.

There is a real sadness when friends decide to leave, especially those who have walked with you for a long time and you have ministered together. In my experience, when leading a small church with a big emphasis on friendship it can be particularly painful. A few years ago when a close friend emailed me to say they were leaving our church, I wrote a little reflection on how it made me feel, to remind me in future times that God is still with me and that I can trust Him. It is a very raw and personal thing but I want to share it with you here in case it is helpful.

When People Leave

When people leave, I feel it first in my stomach. It's like a deep sigh that comes up from my stomach and out of my mouth. I sometimes feel a bit light-headed. I instantly try to shut out the self-recriminations by looking at how positive the leaving message is, but I can't keep that up for long. The questions spray in my face, like cold rain on a windy day, intruding and beating me down. Is this just the slow decline leading to the eventual end of our church? Is this my fault? Why can't we hold on to good people like this who are also our friends? It feels like I am trying to grasp a handful of sand that is slipping through my fingers. Does this prove my time as church leader is done? I set it up but have I stayed in this position too long?

Invariably these things happen at a time when I have just been dreaming up some grand visions and this serves to bring me back down to earth with a bump. How dare I dream, my tired mind teases. How can I be thinking of such exciting things when my core people are leaving because they aren't getting what they need from the church?

The sigh happens again. I distract myself, listening to the radio. Why does this kind of thing hit me so hard? I purse my lips and shake my head. I don't have the answers. Maybe someone else does and I need to let them take this on. Or maybe this is still where God wants me, in the place of great vulnerability.

How will this affect our mission and our giving for LCC? I sigh again. God always provides for us – He always has. But this doesn't make it any easier. I'll have to trust Him for this too. But that can wait till the morning. I need some sleep now. I know I will wake up and when I remember about the email, I will sigh again, and purse my lips and shake my head and ask all the questions again.

I thought we were doing all the things God asked us to do with the church? But it isn't enough. I guess it will never be enough. But God is enough. Tonight I will rest in God. I will trust in Jesus. The Holy Spirit will protect me. Guard my heart and mind in Christ Jesus.[21]

God, please help me to do my best with what You've given me. Help me to lead wisely, to love freely and to serve gladly. I feel so weak and inadequate. But I think that's still where You want me, and where You can use me without me getting in the way quite so much.

So, that is pretty raw! But that is a true summary of how I have felt on a number of occasions over the years. And every time, God has provided. Every time, God has brought new people to encourage and support us. Every time, God has strengthened me. Miracle after miracle, day after day, year after year, through two decades of loving one place and the people who live there.

In this story, Jesus is strengthened by the support of His closest friends, and Peter reaffirms his identity: 'You have the words of eternal life … you are the Holy One of God' (John 6:68-69).

After having thousands of followers and many disciples, Jesus is left with the Twelve and their close friends. And yet, even from that place of weakness, they persevere. They keep following what the Father is doing. They carry on healing the sick and casting out demons and eating with sinners, whether there are 10,000 of them or twelve. And the Holy Spirit continues to perform miracles through them.

There are many examples in the Bible of God showing his strength in our weakness. One of the most famous is

---

[21] See Philippians 4:7.

the story of Gideon in Judges 6. Gideon, who we have already mentioned in this book, is one of the most unwilling leaders in history. An angel calls round to see him and says, 'The LORD is with you, mighty warrior' (Judges 6:12).

Now, what would you say if an angel turned up at your house? I would be pretty scared for starters, then I would listen to *exactly* what the angel said, and then do whatever I was told. Not because I am super-holy but because I would be scared. Plus I would be quite flattered to be called 'mighty warrior'.

Gideon is having none of it. He moans to the angel that God is not very good at showing He is with us. The angel, now referred to as 'the LORD' (v14) is not impressed with Gideon's moaning and tells him to go and save Israel. Gideon is still not impressed with the Lord and tells God how he is from the weakest clan and he is the weakest person in the clan (Judges 6:15). He has no authority to call an army together.

However, the unwilling leader eventually obeys and, with God's authority, gathers an army of more than 30,000 soldiers. But this is too many for God! God wants to show Gideon His power in Gideon's weakness. Through a series of tests, the vast army is whittled down to only 300 people, and yet they win a miraculous victory against overwhelming odds (Judges 7). Gideon is shown that what matters is not how many people you can gather, but whether you are willing to obey God, no matter what the odds.

Sometimes I think of all the need in Salford, all the thousands of people who don't yet know the love of Jesus, and I look at our small church and the other churches in the city, and it seems overwhelming. And yet what is required from us is not might and strength but trust and obedience, in our vulnerability. I meet so many pioneers and church planters who feel like Gideon did – I can't do this, look at who I am, look at the few people I have with me – and I love to remind them (and myself) to, 'Go in the strength you have … Am I not sending you?' (Judges 6:14). God is sending us! He will be our strength! He will fight for us! He is strong in our weakness.

When Jesus sends out the seventy-two, He deliberately sends them out in weakness and dependence: 'Do not take a purse or bag or sandals' (Luke 10:4). He wants them to learn that this is not their mission, but God's mission. He doesn't want them to go to these villages and towns in a position of strength and superiority, but in humility, service and dependence – not just on God's provision but on the kindness of others.

This is not an easy life to live. It is much easier to only go when we feel equipped and well resourced, but from my experience and from the narrative of Scripture, so much of the really exciting and ground-breaking moments come when we go in weakness. The seventy-two return in amazement and joy: 'Lord, even the demons submit to us in your name' (Luke 10:17).

Preaching the gospel, and hearing it back. Obeying the call of God, no matter what the cost. Learning to trust God in times of vulnerability and pain. These are some of the truths we learn from Jesus' life.

In the next chapter we will look at Jesus' teaching – in word and deed – and His death and resurrection.

Chapter Eight
Not Forgotten

I had just finished a seminar. Usually at the end of seminars, people come and thank me for the session, ask a question or occasionally correct me for something they disagreed with. On this occasion I encountered Angry Young Man, who had come to not just correct, but rebuke me. He pushed his way through the nice friendly delegates so he could hear what others were saying. He joined in occasionally when I was trying to answer questions, to ensure the young people were receiving the Correct Doctrines. I took a deep breath, smiled at him and introduced myself.

He was rather angry with the way I had dealt with one of the questions. He was trying to tell me, in a very loud voice, that I had been much too woolly in my answer. I let him be angry, but I did feel that he could find better things to put his passions into than shouting at people for questioning his views.

We got on to discussing (well, him talking and me listening) his views on the teaching at this festival. He basically said that the main meetings were just talks with people telling stories rather than chapter by chapter, verse by verse, expository Bible teaching. I said to him, 'What about Jesus? He didn't seem to do much expository Bible teaching, He mostly told stories.' To his credit, Angry Young Man paused and thought for a moment and admitted he hadn't thought that.

Jesus was a storyteller. His stories were another way of inviting everyone to enter His kingdom. As Eugene Peterson says, 'Stories are verbal acts of hospitality.'[22] Jesus' whole ministry was built around hospitality. His meals with sinners and tax collectors are the most obvious example of this, where He demonstrated by His actions what the kingdom of God looked like. Jesus' table was a place of welcome, but also a place of transformation. People from the edges of society, those rejected and marginalised, were drawn to Jesus and He welcomed them, affirmed them and loved them.

But He didn't just have people come to His table in some kind of charitable act. He was more often the guest than the host, and as He entered into people's homes He also entered into their stories, bringing healing, forgiveness and hope. Jesus' stories had a similar effect – they welcomed His listeners, drawing them in and bringing transformation.

Often people would ask Jesus very straightforward questions, and more often than not he would respond not with a yes or no, or a doctrinal statement, but with a story. I sometimes wonder if I would have got annoyed with Him at times! Just tell us what you think, Jesus – yes or no! 'Well, once upon a time…'

---

[22] Eugene Peterson, *Christ Plays in Ten Thousand Places* (London: Hodder & Stoughton, 2005), p13.

Jesus' stories were ways of helping His listeners to find themselves and their role in the kingdom of God. Some were offended. Some were shocked, others puzzled, but everyone was provoked into a response.

Jesus' actions were communicating His message too – they were *acted parables*. The miracles of Jesus each conveyed a message, whether the feeding of the 5,000, calming the storm, casting out demons, healing the sick or even raising the dead. To use the word mentioned many times in the Gospel of John, all of these were 'signs' of the kingdom.

Jesus did not heal every sick person in the world during His lifetime, although He had the power to do so. He raised Lazarus from the dead (John 11), but as far as we know, Lazarus died again eventually. Jesus fed 5,000 men, but some would have gone hungry the next day. Each of His miracles was a signpost to the kingdom that was coming; each one taught His followers about the nature of God's rule. The miracles were like trailers for a great film, to give people a glimpse, a foretaste, of the fullness of what was to come. This is surely true for us today as well.

We have seen lots of miracles over the years in Langworthy, but we have also prayed many more times and not seen our prayers answered in the way we have wanted them to be. Our job is to follow Jesus – to listen to what God says and to obey. We are to heal the sick and to pray for God's kingdom to come 'on earth as it is in heaven', and that includes all the miracles we see in the New Testament, the spectacular healings as well as the transformed lives and restored relationships, and the radical, generous, faith-filled lifestyle that welcomes all, especially the outcasts.

Jesus communicated His message through His actions, but as the disciples on the road to Emmaus realised, Jesus was 'powerful in *word* and deed' (Luke 24:19, my emphasis). His teaching was, and is, revolutionary. His stories still live in people's imaginations today, whether Christian or not.

One thing that I have noticed in working with pioneers who are ministering in marginalised areas is that the interface between their work and the Bible often comes in two ways – Prophetic Scriptures (we looked at some of them earlier) and Framing Scriptures.

Let me explain what I mean by Framing Scriptures. The Prophetic Scriptures are like vision statements, and as I said earlier, they often come from Isaiah! They give the pioneer something to dream of as an ultimate goal for their community that may never fully come to pass in this age, but that energises them to pray and work for a day when rivers flow in deserts, when the blind see and the deaf hear, when singing is heard throughout the land, when broken buildings are rebuilt and flowers grow in arid places.[23]

The Framing Scriptures, however, give us a way of expressing what we are actually seeing in reality. They help us to have a biblical language to describe the reality of our experiences. Jesus' stories are incredibly helpful in this regard. Let me give you a few examples.

When everything started to unravel in our church, as I described at the start of this book, I found myself scrambling around trying to find some meaning for what was happening. People were leaving, relationships were

---

[23] See Isaiah 35; 54; 61.

falling apart, and our team of leaders was reduced so we couldn't run some of the ministries we had been doing. Others were questioning their faith. Friendships were being strained to breaking point. It wasn't just one situation; there were multiple potential disasters all unfolding at once.

I started to read the parable of the sower (Matthew 13:1-23). As I reflected on this, and not just the current events but the previous two decades, this story helped me to *frame* what I had experienced. First, there is the generosity of the sower. This gospel of Jesus is for everyone.

I was once in a prayer meeting for Salford. I like to encourage whoever is praying with the occasional 'amen' when I agree with them, and maybe a 'mmm' when it's generally good stuff. Anyway, I was doing a few amens and mmms for one person, and then she said something that made me go: 'Mmm, yes, Lord, mmm… eh? No!'

She had said something along the lines of: we pray that we wouldn't waste any time reaching people who are not interested, but only sow in fertile soil. Now, I had to stop giving her any more mmms at that point. The sower sows everywhere. In fact, out of the four areas where the seed goes, three of them are not fertile places – the path, the rocky ground and the place where thorns grow. The sower is generous in the sowing of the gospel, and so should we be.

Imagine if that was the focus of our mission strategy. Let's put three-quarters of our finance into mission into the hardest areas. Let's invest in breaking up the ground in the toughest places. Let's reflect the generosity of Jesus and not just go after the low-hanging fruit with the quick rewards.

Some of the seeds fall on the path and are swallowed by birds. Jesus explains that this is when people hear the word but do not understand it (Matthew 13:19). This is so common, especially when reaching a group of people who know very little about the gospel. When we did an RE week in our local community primary school, we taught them about the Lord's Prayer. In each class we asked if they had ever heard of the Lord's Prayer. Out of 500 children, fewer than twenty-five raised their hands. We realised we were starting near the very beginning in terms of people's knowledge about Jesus and His kingdom. Sometimes we wade in with assumptions about what people know, using our Christian jargon, and it is as if we are speaking a foreign language. They don't understand it, and it gets snatched away.

It can take a long time for people to understand, and during that time it feels as though our message is having no effect at all. It seems like that seed has been taken away by the birds, or, as Jesus says later, by 'the evil one' (Matthew 13:19). We have had a number of people over the years who are part of the church but don't seem to understand the core message of Jesus. Some of them drift away. However, for some, something suddenly happens – an incident in their lives, a moment in a meeting or, somewhat annoyingly, a visiting speaker comes and says everything you've been saying for the past few years, and then the revelation comes! It can be like Paul having scales fall from his eyes (Acts 9:18) – suddenly they see; they understand. We need to be patient with people, to love them, to not despair when they don't 'get it', but to watch what God is doing in their lives and join in with that. Most importantly, keep sowing the seed, because eventually they may be in a place to understand.

The second load of seeds fall on rocky ground (Matthew 13:20). These plants find some soil and grow up quickly, but because of the rocky ground beneath, their roots are not deep enough and the plants are scorched by the sun and wither. We have seen this many times over the years – people respond with joy to the gospel, seem to grow very quickly, but then after a few years when life gets more difficult, their roots are not deep enough to survive. The rocky ground underneath the shallow soil has prevented them from gaining a resilience in their faith.

What is this rocky ground? For us it has been some of the difficulties in people's lives that have held them back. Sometimes it can be difficulties from childhood, or experiences of bereavement that have never been dealt with, or addictions that have held people in their grip. What I have noticed is that when the root grows down and reaches the rocks, this is the key moment.

We often build our lives on the idea that we are basically OK and, with enough determination, we can cope. When that root reaches the hard ground underneath, it is then that we realise we are actually not OK. It is then that God gives us a glimpse of the rocky ground, and invites us to let Him start to break that up, so our roots in Him can go deeper. But it will be painful, and it will involve accepting that we need to change. It might involve confessing sin, or getting professional help, including counselling. In some cases, where the hard ground has come because of bereavement, it may involve being willing to release the deceased person into the hands of

Jesus, rather than trying to hold on to them by constant visits to graves, or, in our community, visits to mediums.

All these things can serve to prevent people from finding the healing that God wants for them. Time does not heal them. Only Jesus can.

So many times, I have seen people who have flourished as young Christians reach this point and draw back. I have seen middle-aged people who still behave like young teenagers, and this can often be traced back to an incident at that age that they never dealt with. They meet Jesus and find some joy and peace, but then can't face allowing God to break up the rocky ground, which means they can never deepen their faith.

The other seeds fall among thorns and grow up but are choked when the thorns grow around them (Matthew 13:22). We were seeing this happen during the difficult time for us as a church – people who had grown up in their faith but were now being strangled by the worries of life. As I reflected on this famous story and how it helped me to frame what we were experiencing, I also asked God, 'But what can we do about this? Where is the hope? What is next?'

I felt God say to me, 'The parable of the sower is not the end of the story.'

The parable of the sower is not the end of the story.

For the person who hears the gospel and doesn't get it, it's not the end of the story.

For the person who responds with joy to the gospel but then their faith withers because of the rocky ground and their roots not being deep enough, it's not the end of the story.

For the person who has come to faith but then finds themselves choked by the worries of life, it's not the end of the story.

It is not the end of your story.

There is hope. In Jesus' kingdom, even when there is death, there is also resurrection. My thoughts went to Simon Peter. He was a Jesus-denier. If they had had social media in those days, he would have gone viral as a Christian leader who had lost his faith. He was deconstructing. 'I don't know him' (Luke 22:57). He even called down curses on himself as he denied the One who had given him new life and hope (Matthew 26:74). He had been choked by the worries of life; he had been scorched by the sun. Had he even fully understood the message? It was all over for him. Jesus was dead, His followers were scattered, and Peter was moving on with his life.

It was not the end for Simon Peter.

It is not the end for you, or for people you know who have denied Jesus.

There is still hope.

Peter would be restored by Jesus, and he would then go on to be one of the key leaders in the early Christian movement as it spread across the known world. His love for Jesus was rekindled in that meeting after Jesus' resurrection, and it was Peter – the Christ-denier, the one whom Jesus called Satan (Matthew 16:23), the one who cursed himself – who stood up and preached that first sermon on the day of Pentecost, when thousands heard the message and decided to follow Jesus for themselves (Acts 2).

When considering Peter's story, I thought of some of my dear friends who were questioning their own faith.

Peter's story gave me hope. I said to God, 'If the parable of the sower isn't the end of the story, what is the next step for us?' I wasn't satisfied with just understanding what had happened – we needed to know what was next.

Instantly I thought about the parable of the prodigal son. This story from Luke 15 is one of the most famous stories in the Bible. The younger son leaves his home and demands his inheritance from his father, in that culture effectively saying to his father, 'I wish you were dead and I want nothing more to do with you.' It would have brought great shame on the family. The wayward son has an empty time pursuing his own lusts until he hits rock bottom and decides to return home. He plans his speech. He will ask his dad for permission to return as a hired servant, as he has effectively forfeited his rights as a son.

What happens next is one of the most beautiful and profound moments in literature. The father, although wronged by the son, is looking, longing for him to return. Jesus tells us, 'While he was still a long way off, his father saw him and was filled with compassion for him' (Luke 15:20). Whenever I read this verse it blows me away. I remember thinking of my own friends who were at that time so far from Jesus – still a long way off – and then realising those two things were true for them as they are for me too: Father God sees you and is full of compassion for you. However far off you might be, whatever dreadful thing you have done or has been done to you, whatever you have said or thought or tweeted, the Father *sees you.* Not only that, He is *full of compassion for you.*

If you will just start to move again towards the Father, see what happens next in the story. The father runs through the village. In that culture, the elders would not run, as it would mean them losing dignity. The father is so full of love and compassion for the son, dignity goes out of the window. And he isn't just running, he is running toward *that son*. The betrayer. The one who brought shame to the family.

When the son sees his dad running, is he afraid? Does he expect to be ushered out of the village in disgrace? Why is he running?

Then the moment comes. The father throws his arms around him and embraces his son. In that moment, the prepared speech becomes irrelevant. All that wasted time, all the pain he has caused, the guilt, the shame, it all melts away in the father's embrace. A party is called for the one who 'was dead and is alive again; he was lost and is found' (Luke 15:24).

I realised when reflecting on this passage that part of our role as church over the following months was to provide more opportunities for those who were 'still a long way off' (v20) to know that the Father sees them, is filled with compassion for them and is running to greet them, and, most importantly, for them to experience the embrace of the Father, where everything else melts away and we are reminded of our true identity as children of God. For the next nine months while we felt unable to put on our Sunday worship gatherings, we came before God again and again in worship and prayer and experienced the compassion-filled embrace of our Father God.

When we emerged from those nine months, we had a renewed focus on meeting with Jesus and inviting others to do so. We relaunched our Sunday gatherings on the fifteenth anniversary of our church, on Easter Sunday. More than half the people who came were visitors, including many who were not regular churchgoers. Sometimes on such occasions I am tempted to play down some of the Christian elements of the service in order to be more accessible to visitors, but this time we were focused on allowing people every opportunity to experience the embrace of the Father. We sang our worship songs to Jesus with passion. I preached about the hope we can find in Jesus. I invited whoever wanted to receive Jesus to come and take communion. I also told them that after they took the bread and wine, one of our team would pray a blessing over them before they returned to their seat.

Almost everyone stood up and came to receive. I was amazed and delighted. One lady asked me if she could go for a blessing because she couldn't take communion – she was a Muslim. I watched as she wept while she was prayed for by our team speaking the love of the Father into her life. It was a wonderful time where so many people met Jesus, and another glimpse for us of what we are called to do. It gave us hope for the future after a devastating year.

I shared some of this story at a conference I was speaking at. I was only visiting for the day, and was thinking, 'Why have I come all this way for one night? I won't be able to get to know people, and what use can one talk be?' The talk was OK, then I led a time of prayer ministry.

I couldn't help but feel there was more that God wanted to do. Then a woman approached me, crying and shaking. She said she'd had a terrible year, and felt a failure. She had been seriously considering giving up, but after what I'd shared about our terrible year, perhaps she could carry on too. I had one of those God moments and looked her in the eye and said, 'You are not a failure.'

At that, she fell on the floor, as the Spirit moved, and as I knelt beside her, praying, I whispered to her, 'I think this is why I came here tonight, for you.' She nodded in reply.

After a while I got up and spoke to the whole meeting again and said, 'If you have come here feeling like you're a failure and you want to give up, please come forward for prayer.' Probably about 100 people responded, and as I told them, 'You are not a failure,' it felt as if all heaven had broken out. This is why God had wanted me there. To tell a bunch of tired urban missionaries that they had not failed, that they could carry on, and even though they had felt a long way off, the Father saw them and was filled with compassion for them, and in that moment He embraced us all and gave us hope for the future. This is what God does. It is beautiful.

The parable of the prodigal son is the last of three parables about lost things in Luke 15. The first parable is about a lost sheep. The shepherd leaves the ninety-nine to find the one lost sheep, and when he returns he throws a party to celebrate its return. The second story is about a woman who loses a coin. She then sweeps through the whole house until she finds it, then she too has a party with her family and friends. One of the key things we notice in the three 'lost' parables in Luke 15 is the celebration at the end of each story. Each one involves friends and family being invited round and a feast with joy and dancing.

I think this is fascinating, and quite countercultural if we try to apply it to our day. The lost son is the most dramatic example – all this fuss over a rebel who shamed the family. The other two stories are also quite strange. A big party for one sheep in a hundred? Even more so, inviting all your friends and family round to celebrate you finding... one coin? But this is the wonder of the kingdom. There is 'rejoicing in heaven over one sinner who repents' (v7). The angels join in with the heavenly party! There is a huge celebration for just one person.

In a world, and even a church, often obsessed with numbers, this is a healthy challenge. Some would look at the parties for the one and be tempted to say, 'Why are you having a party for just one coin/sheep?' But the kingdom of Jesus spreads in this way – through a demon-possessed man who lived in a tomb (Mark 5:1-20), or a woman who had been labelled as unclean for twelve years (Mark 5:25-34). Jesus goes to the ones and twos – He seeks them out – He gets a boat across the lake to see the man known as Legion, then immediately sends him as a missionary back to his village (Luke 8:26-39). He walks to the margins where the lepers live, and heals them (Luke 17:11-19).

This is the Jesus way. We can invent our own ways that might produce quicker results, but the Jesus way is to reach the ones and twos – the person serving us in the supermarket, the elderly neighbour, the parent at the school gate, the homeless person outside the coffee shop. Jesus stopped for the one. The shepherd left all the other sheep to look for the one. The woman turned her house upside down looking for the one. The father lost all his dignity in the community running towards and embracing the one. There are a tiny minority of Christians who are called to and gifted in reaching large amounts of people all at once. Most of us – in fact, all of us – need to look at who is in front of us. One person at a time. Love them, pray for them, show them the love of Jesus, listen to their story and humbly offer our own.

This is how Jesus works. He leaves the crowds behind and goes after the one. He allows a woman who is bleeding to interrupt him when the crowds want him to perform for them. Just when He is becoming successful and massive crowds are following Him, he starts saying weird things about eating his flesh and drinking his blood, and the big numbers fade away and he's left with the ones who have nowhere else to go.

The losers, the uneducated, the traitors, the terrorists. The ones He called by name. Peter, Andrew, Martha, Matthew, Mary, James, John, Joanna, Judas. He loves them and He knows them. He found them. He turned from the crowds and went after them.

In the UK we had eighteen months of lockdown restrictions when churches were not allowed to gather big crowds. We were stuck in our houses, with only our nearest neighbours available to see 'in person'. Some churches celebrated their social media views on YouTube, and this may have had some impact. We want as many as possible to hear about Jesus, but ultimately 99,000 viewers on my viral video is nothing compared to the party in heaven for Gordon, who we mentioned earlier in the book. A lost pensioner who was found, and is now embraced by Jesus forever.

Let us repent of our desire for big crowds and the lie of success measured by numbers, and use this time to name the people we are reaching and searching for. Let us redefine success in God's kingdom as nothing more and nothing less than faithfulness to Jesus.

Until we do that, it's hard to go crazy and have a wild party and rejoice over the one who is found – just *one* person? He's a bit old and not very influential! Lord, free us from the idolatry of numbers and let us see the ones and the twos. Let us find the treasures hidden in the fields. Let us search with the urgency of the shepherd, or the woman looking for her coin. Let us watch with the compassionate intensity of the father, looking for those who are still far off.

Let me tell you about my friend Joe. Joe came along to the church I grew up in, and was a few years younger than me. He had a twin brother, but the two of them were quite different. His brother was outgoing, eloquent and confident, an obvious leader who began to experience God in his early teens. Joe was quieter and his posture was very different – he was usually slouched with his head down, as if acknowledging that he was overshadowed by his brother, looking like he was carrying the weight of the world on his shoulders. Their mum brought the lads to church but we didn't see much of their dad. It turns out that neither did they.

Joe's experience of his father was primarily one of absence – his dad struggled with addiction, especially to alcohol, and would often disappear for long periods. Joe would also feel the force of his drunken rages at times.

It was at our church that Joe would gain positive male role models. Men who were devoted to prayer and loved Jesus, who took an interest in him, who noticed him and invested in him.

I remember praying for Joe when he was in his early teens and being reminded of the story of David being anointed by Samuel, when his brothers were the obvious candidates and yet he was chosen as king (1 Samuel 16:1-13). I knew Joe was learning to play the guitar and asked him if he would like to lead a song or two at our youth meetings.

I didn't have a clue at the time how significant this would be for Joe. I didn't know how difficult things were at home. I didn't know how utterly worthless he felt, how he felt overlooked and forgotten about. I didn't know that as his brother was having amazing encounters with the Holy Spirit, Joe was struggling because he wasn't feeling God's presence, and was even wondering if God had forgotten about him, whether God had just noticed his brother and not him.

I remember the thirteen-year-old Joe leading us in a song of worship. It was slightly shaky but there was a sense of God's presence with us in that moment and I knew that this would be a part of his calling. Just as David was a worshipper and songwriter who had been forgotten about by people but not by God, Joe had also been given a voice to lead people and an ability to write songs.

It was a joy and privilege over the next few years to play a small part in Joe gaining in confidence in his calling, finding some healing from the past and going on to lead people in worship in churches, schools and conferences.

It was a rocky road for Joe. Not everything changed in those moments at the age of thirteen. His story is unfinished, but I am so proud of him in the way that he has persevered through tough times and been open to God changing him, and the ability he has to honestly reflect on the ups and downs of his life.

People often ask me what it takes to raise up 'indigenous leaders' from estates like ours, and I think of

Joe when asked that question. A local lad, who could have gone off the rails with anger, insecurities and hopelessness, he has remained faithful to his call from God and gone through a real formation process that is still ongoing, and God has blessed so many people through his life, his songs and his story.

When I asked Joe what the key factors were in this whole process, he emphasised the importance of finding in church strong, godly male role models and mentors, having people who believed in him and took a risk on him, and experiencing God in worship. There are all things that helped to break up the hard ground in his life, revealing the fertile soil, producing much fruit.

There are so many stories Joe told me about seemingly insignificant moments – inviting him to a worship event, asking him to lead a Bible study, encouraging him in his guitar playing – that actually made a huge difference in his life. A kid with no confidence in himself found that he was loved, noticed and needed. The overlooked, quiet twin realised he was not forgotten. Joe is one of God's treasures.

Jesus told another parable about treasure, about a man who found a treasure in a field, then went and sold everything he had to buy it (Matthew 13:44). Claudia in Stenhouse talks about their calling as a kind of treasure hunting – searching it out like the lost coin, and when they find it, it's worth more than anything. This is such a great way to look at mission, especially in the more difficult places, because often the first thing people look at is the needs of the area, and how they can be met. If you are a treasure hunter, you're looking for what is beautiful and precious. You are looking, expecting to find it. You don't look and just see high crime rates and social problems; you look deeper to find the treasures hidden there.

Jesus talks about seeking the kingdom of God (Matthew 6:33), and we need to keep our eyes open to see what is hidden in these places. In His Sermon on the Mount, He told His listeners that the road to life is narrow, and not many find it (Matthew 7:14). If it is the case that not many find it, we need to look in places that not many are looking in! Both Moses and John the Baptist found it in the wilderness. The prophet Samuel found it when he went beyond the older, stronger brothers and into the shepherd's field to find young David. Time and time again we have found the treasures of God's kingdom in the most unexpected places.

The other important detail in this parable is that the man realised that the treasure he had found was worth selling all he had in order to have it. I want to end this chapter with a plea to you. Please orient your entire life around Jesus. If it means selling everything you own and giving it away, just do it. If it means stopping one job to do something else, go for it. If it might mean you'll be embarrassed or disapproved of by others, just do it anyway. I'm forty-six now, which is a bit of a surprise to me, but if there is one thing that I have learned over those four and a half decades it is this: there is nothing and no one better than Jesus. Jesus is the treasure that it is worth looking everywhere for. Jesus is the pearl of 'great value' (Matthew 13:45-46). Jesus is wonderful and trustworthy and utterly faithful and kind and loving and better than any words that any of us could ever come up with.

When I was ten and went to the Spring Harvest conference and realised that God wasn't just a story in the

Bible but a person to be loved, and who loves, that was when I first realised that nothing is better than Jesus.

When I was thirteen and had an experience of the Holy Spirit filling me for the first time, I was so utterly overwhelmed and excited that I literally ran around Butlin's in Minehead, Somerset, jumping up and down! I was reminded that nothing is better than Jesus.

When I was in my late teens I ended an unhealthy relationship with a girlfriend, because I felt God had told me to. I experienced a peace and assurance of God in my life that has literally never left me. I remember walking away from that hard conversation with someone I really liked, somehow full of Jesus' presence. I was reminded again that nothing is better than Jesus.

When I was eighteen and I stood outside our church with my friends, having just put my twenty-one-year-old cousin's coffin in the hearse, and we got into a circle and cried and prayed desperate prayers for God to help us, I made a solemn decision that Jesus had the words of eternal life and I had nowhere else to go (John 6:68). Since that moment I have had no doubt that I will be with Jesus when I die, and I have tried to live every day for Jesus. Nothing is better than Jesus.

When I was thirty and my wife, Esther, was rushed into emergency surgery as our first child, Daniel, was being born and I had ten minutes of hell in a tiny room on my own that felt like ten years, with every thought coming into my head of the worst possible things that could happen, I prayed and gave them both to Jesus, because even in that dark moment I remembered that I had nowhere else to go. He was the only one I could trust then, and I knew Jesus was with me.

Whatever you are going through today, Jesus has the words of eternal life. There is nothing better that you could do right now than put all your trust in Jesus. There is nothing better than Him.

We are in a world emerging from a global pandemic, and we feel a strange pressure to leap into this new world with enthusiasm and vision, but actually we are all really tired and feeling a bit guilty for feeling tired and not having much vision or enthusiasm for the new world! What I need to say to you today – *takes a breath* – is that Jesus has the words of eternal life.

I will never write anything that is as important as this: give your whole life to Jesus today. Throw yourself into the adventure that is God's kingdom, following Jesus each day, empowered by His Spirit. In all the things I have been through, it has been knowing Jesus and being known by Him that has been central to it all. This has brought me meaning, hope, perseverance, joy and peace. Nothing is better than Jesus.

Chapter Nine
The Cross

The night before He died, Jesus had supper with His friends. As was typical in His ministry, a key moment in His teaching took place at the dinner table.

People from all over the world had come to Jerusalem to celebrate Passover. They told the great story of the Exodus from Egypt, when God freed them from slavery, gave them the Law and eventually led them into the Promised Land. Each part of the Passover meal had a meaning, as they ate and retold their great founding stories. They remembered together, but it was not an ordinary type of remembering. None of them had been there for the actual Exodus, which had happened many centuries before. This was a type of reliving the story, of inhabiting the story again. They would own the story. It's a bit like when you have old friends round and you tell the hilarious stories that formed your friendships, and you can almost smell and taste them again. You feel the same emotions you felt then; you aren't just calling them to mind, but actually reliving them. This is the kind of *experiential* remembrance we are talking about here. Not that they had personal memories of the Exodus, but they entered into the story and it became their own as they ate and drank together.

It was in this context that Jesus took bread and wine and identified them with His body and blood, which would soon be broken and 'poured out' for them (Matthew 26:26-29). He gave the meal a new meaning. This meal would still be about freedom and Exodus, but about the exodus that Jesus Himself would accomplish as the new Moses (see Luke 9:31) – a freedom from sin and evil and death. He instructed His followers to do this 'in remembrance' (Luke 22:19) of Him – in remembrance of the freedom He would bring, in remembrance of His blood 'poured out for many for the forgiveness of sins' (Matthew 26:28).

For the first few years after Jesus' death, the earliest Christians would gather around their meal tables and retell the stories about Jesus – His life, teaching, miracles, death and resurrection. During these meals they would take bread, give thanks, break it and share it together. Then they would take a cup of wine and share that together. As they did that, three things were happening

. They were remembering what had happened in the past – the cross and resurrection, when the world changed forever and the power of death was defeated.

Second, they looked forward to the glorious future, when God's kingdom would come in all its fullness at Jesus' return. Paul had taught them that whenever they ate the bread and drank from the cup, they proclaimed Jesus' death '*until he comes*' (1 Corinthians 11:26, my emphasis).

The third thing was that they were actually encountering the risen Jesus in that moment. It wasn't just an old story, and it wasn't just a future hope. The power of the cross and resurrection was present with them at their meal. The glorious future promise was visiting them in that moment. As they retold the story, they entered into the story themselves, receiving forgiveness and freedom again, being healed and empowered by the Holy Spirit as the risen Jesus fed them.

We can do this in our day. Just as the earliest Jesus followers knew His presence at their meals, we can do the same. Some of the most profound moments in our church over the years have come as we have shared bread and wine together. I shared earlier about the freedom that our friend Gordon found when he realised that Jesus invites everyone to His table, no matter what they have done.

I will never forget that day. I remember being close to tears looking down that queue of people waiting to receive, each one of them dearly loved by God. There was a person who was consumed by grief, coming to receive healing. There was another struggling with serious addictions, desperate for a new start but feeling trapped and helpless. There was a young person who only occasionally came to church who ran to be first to receive, finding themselves drawn to Jesus' invite to the table. Each of them in need, each of them welcome.

I needed to receive too. I was tired and weary. The cross brought us together.

On another occasion someone who had been attending church for some weeks but had kept us at arm's length took the bread and wine and said it was the first time in their life that they felt they belonged anywhere.

As we eat and drink and remember Jesus, we enter into His story again. We experience His presence again. We receive hope for the future as we remember the past, and are given strength for today.

A friend of mine, Anna, works in healthcare, in an amazing organisation that provides good-quality healthcare in poorer areas where it has been lacking. She was working at a Covid vaccination centre, and her job that day was to squirt sanitiser into people's hands as they went into the centre. Anna looked down this long queue of people, all over seventy, many of whom hadn't been out of their houses for months. As she put the sanitiser into their hands and looked into their eyes, she saw their hope for the future. Hope that they might be able to hug their grandchildren again, hope that they might not die yet, hope that they could go to the shops safely once more. Anna was reminded of serving the bread and wine at a Soul Survivor festival to hundreds of queuing young people, each coming to receive from Jesus, each of them with an unknown future, but being drawn to the hope that is offered.

Anna was also aware that each person was taking the vaccine for themselves but also for everyone else, just as we come to Jesus' table to receive for ourselves, but also that we might share His love with others. For Anna, this was a tiny glimpse of the kingdom of God. A signpost in a dark time that all will be well.

The vaccines are a remarkable achievement that will save many lives. But that moment was just a hint of what it means when we share bread and wine together in the presence of the risen Jesus. We are reminding ourselves that there is healing coming for every disease. There is forgiveness available for every sin. There will be peace for every nation. The creation itself will be healed. As Julian of Norwich famously said, 'All shall be well, and all manner of things shall be well.'[24] We get glimpses of this when we share bread and wine together at Jesus' table.

When Jesus hung on the cross, absorbing into Himself everything that the fallen world could throw at Him – the political terror, the religious corruption, the evil spiritual powers – He chose to love and forgive, even as people hurled insults at Him. He showed a different way to live, to love, and now, to die. Most of His disciples had scattered. Judas had betrayed Him and the rest were in hiding, fearing for their lives. Only some of the women who had followed Him, including His mother, Mary, had remained, as well as the one known as the 'Beloved Disciple' – 'the disciple whom [Jesus] loved' (John 19:25-26).

Mary had been there at the start and she was there at the end. She watched as her son was mocked, as He hung there in agony. All that emerged from Him was love and forgiveness. As Jesus breathed His last, darkness came over the land. The Saviour was dead.

Imagine that evening. Did any of them sleep? Mary would have remembered the prophecies about a sword piercing her soul as she lay there, crushed by grief (Luke 2:35). Peter would have been wracked by guilt. Judas ended his own life. Perhaps the disciples might have drifted off to sleep and then, on Saturday morning, had that brief moment on waking where it seemed like just another day, until the events of Friday came hurtling into their minds again.

---

[24] Julian of Norwich, *Revelations of Divine Love* (London: Penguin Classics, 1998), p27.

What would that day, that Holy Saturday, have felt like as Jesus' body lay in the tomb? Did some of the disciples get together to talk? 'It's all over. I can't believe it. We were so convinced He was the Messiah. All those miracles He did! There was something so special about Him. How did we get it so wrong?'

The confusion must have been overwhelming for them. We know the story now, 2,000 years later, but in the darkness of Holy Saturday, Jesus' followers didn't have a clue that something was happening that would defeat the power of death forever.

One Easter weekend, an atheist TV historian reminded her followers that dead people do not return to life![25] The truth is, everyone, including Christians, know that this is true. In fact, the followers of Jesus in the first century also knew that dead people don't come back to life. That is why what happened on Easter Sunday was rather a shock. And it is also why, on Holy Saturday, no one was thinking, 'Maybe He'll come back from the dead tomorrow.' They were all devastated. They had to accept He was not the One they had hoped He was. And perhaps that was even worse than the grief of losing their friend.

All over the world, millions of people have lost loved ones in the pandemic, and many have been robbed of the chance to be present at their funerals and grieve as they wanted or needed to. There has also been increased anxiety about illness and death, with many people being afraid to leave their houses. Holy Saturday is so important in these times, because on that day Jesus experienced what

---

[25] www.twitter.com/theAliceRoberts/status/1378037531632091137 (accessed 12th October 2021).

humans fear the most: death. He experienced for Himself the curse of humanity. In doing this, He fully identified with our human experience. As Michael Lloyd says, 'His love did not just bring him to walk with us along the sunny lanes of Galilee: it brought him to lie inert alongside us on the sunless shelf of the grave.'[26] As a result of this, says Lloyd, 'The grave is no longer a place of despair, but a bed of hope. It need no longer be a terminus, but a tunnel.'[27]

Over the years in our estate in Langworthy, I have met so many people who are consumed by grief, in such a way that it controls their lives and often pushes them towards spiritualists, which further traps them in a cycle of grief and dependence. The story of Holy Saturday offers us an alternative way to approach death.

When I was eighteen I was in a band with my two cousins and another friend. We were very keen to tell our mates about Jesus, but we only knew three songs, so we would invite our friends to gigs, play our three songs, then have a preacher talk about Jesus for half an hour, then we would repeat one of the songs to end. Weirdly, some people actually became Christians and are still following Jesus today!

We were all very close friends and did everything together. My cousin Anthony was our keyboard player. He was three years older than me but way cooler. You know, that kind of lad who is good at sport, amazing at music, just a lovely guy and all the girls like him? That was

---

[26] Michael Lloyd, *Café Theology* (London: Alpha International, 2006), p197.
[27] Ibid, p198.

Anthony. I wanted to be like him. At one point he learned to play the flute. Not cool at all, but somehow he pulled it off, and so I booked flute lessons. I had one lesson and it didn't go well. Anyway, you get the idea. I used to go and visit him at Swansea University where he studied. He was clever as well and was one of those kids who did Further Maths like it was a normal thing to do.

One Sunday evening, on the weekend of his twenty-first birthday, I was at church in Salford when we had a phone call to say Anthony had gone missing. He had been out for his birthday the night before but they couldn't find him the next day. I remember just thinking, 'He'll be fine, he'll turn up.' When we got the phone call to say his body had been found in the sea, I didn't know what to do.

A bunch of people ended up at our church, crying, praying and just being devastated together. Why would God let this happen? What about all the plans we had? How would we ever be able to carry on with our lives?

The next few weeks were a blur. I would see someone who wore similar clothes and think it was him. I had dreams where we were talking together but then woke up to the crushing realisation that it wasn't real. I watched friends pull away from church, not knowing how to process their grief and where God was in it all.

One incident helped me during this time.

After a few months I was in a worship event where a big crowd had gathered to hear a well-known Christian worship leader. I was sitting next to my dad, and as we sang together there was a pause in the music. The backing singer got out a recorder. Now, my dad really doesn't like the recorder. The worship leader said that the backing singer was going to prophesy over us using the recorder.

(We used to do things like this in the charismatic world of the 1990s.) I could feel my dad wince at the prospect of prophecy through a recorder. Surely it must be unbiblical.

I closed my eyes, partly to stop myself laughing, as the woman began to play. Suddenly I had this feeling of God's presence with me. I felt God say, 'You are blaming Me for Anthony's death.' Into my mind came this vision of Anthony in a big green field, running and jumping and laughing. I felt God go on, 'I haven't taken anything away from him; I have given him everything.'

I knew that Anthony was with Jesus, in the best possible place he could be, and I also knew that when I die, I will join him there; I will be with Jesus too, and maybe me and Anthony can kick a football together in that big field.

Right then, I was able to release Anthony into Jesus' hands. This was a huge moment in receiving healing. I hadn't wanted to let him go. I wanted him back with me – that was why I was having those dreams, and mistakenly seeing him in crowds. As I released him to Jesus, I started to cry again, but this time they were tears of joy, knowing that he was experiencing the greatest joy any human could ever imagine, and way more than that.

On that day, I was changed permanently. I had no more bitterness about what had happened. Anthony had twenty-one years on this earth. I realised that every single minute of every day was a gift from God. I resolved to use that passion and emotion as a creative force to propel me into living every day for Jesus. I've had twenty-five more years than he had so far, and I have tried to honour his memory by living all out for Jesus.

If you are experiencing the kind of grief that has trapped you and is consuming you, I want to say that Jesus is utterly trustworthy. Your friend or family member who has died cannot be brought back to you – not through your efforts, not through a mystical experience, not through a medium. The way that you can find healing and best honour their memory is to release them into the hands of Jesus.

I know of Christians who are grieving people who were apparently not Christians when they died. This can be especially difficult, and I know some who say, 'If she is not going to be in heaven, I'm not sure I want to be either.' This is not a book for a debate on what happens when you die, but I can honestly say that you can trust Jesus with them too.

Let me tell you one other story.

When I was at school there was a kid in my class who was bullied. She was a scruffy-looking kid who was socially awkward and an easy target for the bullies. I had been to a Christian youth event where they had told us that if Jesus was in our class at school, He would befriend the kid no one else liked, and so should we. So, fired up to follow Jesus, I started sitting next to her in class, attempting to impose my friendship upon her in Jesus' name. She was pretty annoying, actually, and she was into witchcraft so she used to draw pentagrams on the desk and try to cast spells on me. I just muttered a few Bible verses in reply and the spells didn't seem to have any effect.

Then I started to try to Bible bash her, telling her she was going to hell, that kind of stuff, as a good evangelical! I would throw in Bible verses in an attempt to convince/scare her: 'There is a way that appears to be right, but in the end it leads to death' (Proverbs 14:12)! She eventually stopped her occult ways to become a Buddhist, which I thought was a bit of an improvement. Then months later she told me she believed in Jesus like I did! I was delighted for a minute, until she said, 'This guy gave me a copy of *The Watchtower* magazine, and God told me it was true!' and I realised she had become a Jehovah's Witness. Anyway, we became good friends. In fact, she told me years later that I was one of only three people in her childhood who she could call a friend. She managed to forgive my dreadful attempts at evangelism, and I forgave the spells.

Over the years we lost touch, but then connected again through the wonder of social media. She had got back into the occult, after being kicked out of the Jehovah's Witnesses for bad behaviour. I asked her what had been going on during those teenage years – why did she act like that? What was behind the constant search for spiritual experiences? She then told me about some terrible incidents from her past that she had suffered within her family, and the pain when that went on throughout her teenage years, as well as all the bullying she had to endure at school. She thanked me for my friendship, one of her few constants during those years, and for my prayers for her. I prayed again for her.

It was after a few months of not hearing from my friend (she lived elsewhere in the country) that I heard via a family member that she had taken her own life. As I grieved for her and prayed for her family and friends, and reflected on her life, including my unhelpful attempts at evangelism, I wondered about what had happened to her when she died. She was never a Christian. The more I prayed, the more I was utterly convinced that in my own grief, I could utterly trust her into the hands of Jesus. It is Jesus who died for her. It is Jesus who knew her life story, the abuse, the bullying, the search for meaning in religion and sex. It is Jesus who saw my feeble attempts to give her the good news of the gospel.

Thankfully it is not up to me to decide what happens to her eternally. But I do know for sure that I can totally trust Jesus that it will be the most just, loving, merciful and true outcome. I know that when I see Jesus face to face and ask Him, I will say, 'Of course! Of course, that is the best possible thing that could have happened.' Jesus went to the grave, His dead body lay there, to make a way for all of us. Because of this I know for certain that all who know Jesus will spend eternity with Him. I don't know all the answers about what happens to others like my dear friend, but I do know I can utterly trust Jesus.

I pray that as the church of Jesus we can bring this good news to everyone we meet. I pray that people will find healing from the destructive power of the twisted type of grief that controls many, and from the overwhelming fear of death. This is the good news of Holy Saturday. We know someone who has been there before us. And that person, by His Spirit, can live in our lives today.

Holy Saturday is not the end of the story.

Chapter Ten
Resurrection

Have you ever felt like you just can't go on? Like you can't see a way forward? Like it is just too hard? In my role as a leader at our church, the most common lie that has entered my head over the years is, 'You can't do this.' It takes different forms, like, 'You don't have what it takes,' or, 'You aren't really living this out as you should,' or, 'You are not good enough.' It happens most often just in my head, usually after a church meeting that hasn't gone exactly as I had hoped. Sometimes it comes through the words of well-meaning friends, including church members, as they give their opinions about the way I have led something or decisions I have made.

In those darker moments, it is important to remember first that God is with us in the darkness, but also that at any moment, change could happen. As the disciples went to bed on the evening of Holy Saturday, they could never have imagined what was about to happen.

In the Gospels we read that Mary Magdalene and some of the other women who followed Jesus go to His tomb with spices for the body, only to find it empty. Peter and John then go to the tomb and also find it empty. As we saw earlier, the risen Jesus chooses to appear first to Mary and appoints her as the apostle to the apostles, the first bringer of the good news of His resurrection. As He speaks her name in that garden, she becomes the first witness of the New Creation.

Over the next forty days, Jesus appears to many more people. He eats meals with them and allows them to touch His hands and feet and side (John 20:27). He prays with them and does even more miracles, and forgives and reinstates Peter (John 21). Then He disappears again, promising that He will return, but in the meantime they should wait in Jerusalem for the gift of the Holy Spirit (Acts 1:4).

What do we mean by resurrection? Was Jesus a ghost? Was it a heavenly vision? Was it a mass delusion? Did they actually just meet Jesus 'in their hearts' and not in reality? That is not the story that the Bible tells. Let's think a bit more about resurrection.

When Jesus visited Jerusalem, He would stay with some of his friends in Bethany, just outside Jerusalem. The sisters Mary and Martha and their brother Lazarus would have become close to Jesus over the years and known about His miracles. Lazarus became very ill and the sisters sent word to Jesus to come. Jesus delayed His visit, and Lazarus died. When Jesus finally arrived at the house, His friend had been in a tomb for four days. As Jesus approached the house, Martha came to meet him, distraught with grief and clearly angry with Jesus. 'Lord … if you had been here, my brother would not have died' (John 11:21). Jesus told her that Lazarus would rise again, and Martha agreed: 'I know he will rise again in the resurrection at the last day' (John 11:24).

Martha knew that, according to her beliefs, the righteous dead would rise again in a glorious day when God would put the world to rights again, a day that many people called 'The Resurrection'. Isaiah talked about a banquet when death would be swallowed up forever, and God would renew the heavens and the earth (Isaiah 25:6-8). On this day of resurrection, the dead would rise to be judged, as Daniel prophesied: 'Multitudes who sleep in the dust of the earth will awake' (Daniel 12:2). So Martha didn't need Jesus to tell her that Lazarus would rise again, she already knew it would happen at 'The Resurrection'.

What was Jesus' reply? Something that would blow her mind forever: 'I am the resurrection and the life' (John 11:25). Imagine Martha's reaction here. This man, this friend of hers who has stayed in her house, this miracle worker, teacher and prophet, is standing in front of her and saying that *He* is the resurrection! That in some way, all those glorious promises for the future about the dead rising and a New Creation being made and every tear being wiped away and peace coming to the earth and death itself being swallowed up forever at the great banquet – somehow, that future is standing in front of her in the person of her friend, Jesus of Nazareth. The future has come to visit her in the present day, standing in front of her in flesh and blood. She doesn't know it yet, but this is the person by whom and in whom 'all things were created' (Colossians 1:16). Being a few days late to heal her brother is not a major issue for Him.

And so the One who called the worlds into being now calls the name of Lazarus. The One who would gently speak the name of Mary in the garden of New Creation calls with all the authority of the Creator God just three words: 'Lazarus, come out!' (John 11:43).

Lazarus is dead. But dead people don't rise again. Lazarus' rotting body stinks. Lazarus walks out of the tomb. How could he not? The One who is later called 'the Alpha and the Omega' (Revelation 22:13), 'the First and the Last' (Revelation 1:17) – His words carry all the authority. Death trembles at His words. He is giving us another glimpse of the future, when death will be swallowed up forever.

But what happens to Lazarus is not 'The Resurrection'. Lazarus will die again. His body is still flesh and blood, perishable. Lazarus has been miraculously resuscitated by Jesus, like an extreme version of someone whose heart has stopped and is revived by a defibrillator.

But what happens to Jesus Himself is the first resurrection. Jesus' body has not just woken up again. Equally, He hasn't just received a new body while the old one is left to decay. The tomb is empty. God the Father has begun the New Creation. The body of Jesus, which was broken and bloodied and has in some way carried the sin of the world, has been healed and renewed but made into something much more glorious. It is a physical body but it has new properties that enable Jesus to appear and disappear at will, and to avoid being recognised until He chooses.

The first Easter Sunday is the first day of the new week of creation.

The apostle Paul tells us that Jesus' resurrected body is 'the firstfruits' (1 Corinthians 15:20) of this New Creation that God is bringing about. From that point onwards, every person who believes and trusts in the resurrected

Jesus gets to be a part of this movement: 'if anyone is in Christ, the new creation has come: the old is gone, the new is here!' (2 Corinthians 5:17).

Before Jesus ascends to heaven, He commissions His New Creation people to take this message of freedom, hope and rebirth all over the world. Everyone needs to hear the good news, to have the opportunity to be a part of this New Creation project. In Revelation 21:5 Jesus says, 'I am making everything new!', and it is with this mission that all Jesus followers are invited to join in – a mission to see the world renewed – individuals forgiven and restored, relationships reconciled, nations experiencing perfect peace and the creation itself being healed and renewed. But it will take an empowered people to see this happen.

Jesus tells His disciples to wait in Jerusalem for the gift of the Holy Spirit (Luke 24:49), when they will receive power to be His witnesses 'to the ends of the earth' (Acts 1:8).

In an upper room, with their Lord no longer physically present with them, while their fellow Jews gather in the city to celebrate the feast of Pentecost and tell the stories of the giving of the Law in the storm on Mount Sinai, a heavenly storm enters the room (Acts 2:1-4). A sound like a violent wind is heard. Peter looks over at John and sees what looks like a tongue of fire on his head. As he looks around the room, the same has happened to all of them. Just like the storm with wind and fire on Sinai (Exodus 19:16-19), a new law is being given in this storm, being written in their minds and on their hearts as Jeremiah prophesied centuries earlier (Jeremiah 31:31-34).

Each of the people in the room begins to speak in a language they have not learned before, reversing the curse of Babel (Genesis 11), and as they spill out into the square, loudly proclaiming the wonders of God, a huge crowd gathers (Acts 2:5-6).

Empowered by the Spirit, Peter stands up and tells the story of Jesus. Everyone there knows that dead people don't rise again. But 3,000 of them find themselves believing that one man – Jesus of Nazareth – has risen. They will then return to their own countries with this strange and compelling message of resurrection, New Creation and the kingdom of God, only to find that many more people will believe it when they retell the stories.

Not only do people believe, but the same miracles that Jesus performed still happen when they pray in Jesus' name. People are healed, demons are cast out and the outcasts find a place at the table. The world is changing. Jesus is 'making everything new'.

The earliest Church didn't just perform miracles and speak about the Jesus story. They lived lives of unusual purity and astounding generosity – not considering any of their possessions as their own, but freely sharing everything. They lived in the spirit of the ancient practice of Jubilee in their own day (Leviticus 25). Acts tells us that 'there was no needy person among them' (Acts 4:34). This is not to say that they didn't allow poor people to join them, but once a part of the community, they were no longer poor because of the generosity of their new Christian family. When persecution came, the Christians were noted for their patience in hard times.

It was often the lifestyle of the earliest Christians that was the greatest witness to those around them. Lesslie

Newbigin famously said that the Church is 'the only hermeneutic of the gospel'.[28] By this he meant that people will best understand our message by the lives that we live. At its best, the Church is the place where we show people what the gospel looks like in practice. Jesus said, 'Let your light shine before others, that they may see your good deeds and glorify your Father in heaven' (Matthew 5:16).

My friend Judy, who leads Barton Community Church near Oxford, tells the story of a person who joined their church and after a while said that no one had loved them like that church did. That church, which has just celebrated ten years in that estate, is demonstrating what the gospel looks like in practice.

A couple of years ago I preached at a church in the Anfield area of Liverpool. As a fervent Manchester United fan, I was slightly nervous going into the heart of enemy territory. When I arrived I looked around the room, and it was an incredibly eclectic group of people. The church works in the red-light district and some of the women they worked with were attending. There was a large group from the Iranian community, lots of kids and teenagers sitting near a couple of rows of elderly people, and on the front row some huge blokes who looked like gangsters.

As I stood up to preach, the vicar introduced me: 'This is Chris Lane, and he is a Man United fan!' I had hoped to remain undercover. I wondered if I would survive the meeting.

I looked again at this diverse group and said, 'This is a proper church. Look at you all. There is no way a group of

[28] Lesslie Newbigin, *The Gospel in a Pluralist Society* (London: SPCK, 1989), p227.

people like this would all be in the same room if it wasn't for a miracle.'

It was true. That church was a miracle. It is only Jesus that could bring them all together. That church was a glimpse of the New Creation. I'm sure it had its faults, but in its own way it was a hermeneutic of the gospel. I could take someone there and say, 'This is what Jesus does.'

Leaders in the early Church used to point to this diversity and to the patience, miracles and generosity of the churches as evidence of the truth of the gospel. Here are some quotes from three prominent writers in the first three centuries of the Church:

> Tertullian: 'The things which make us luminaries of the world are these – our good works.'[29]

> Origen: Churches are 'evidences of Jesus' divinity'.[30]

> Minucius Felix: 'As for the daily increase in our numbers, that is no proof of errors but evidence of merit, for beauty of life encourages its followers to persevere, and strangers to join the ranks.'[31]

---

[29] Tertullian, 'On the Apparel of Women', www.newadvent.org/fathers/0402.htm (accessed 12th October 2021).
[30] Origen, 'Against Celsus 3:33', www.newadvent.org/fathers/04163.htm (accessed 12th October 2021).
[31] Minicius Felix, 'Octavius', https://www.loebclassics.com/view/minucius_felix-octavius/1931/pb_LCL250.413.xml (accessed 6th January 2022).

Think about your own church. Where are there glimpses of the New Creation? Where do you see healing, forgiveness, reconciliation, creation care, peace-making, joy, community, generosity, kindness and patience? Tell those stories to each other. Build a culture of storytelling. Over the past couple of years in our church we have had a time every week where we ask people what God has done in the past few days. This prevents us from relying on old stories and creates an expectation that God will be at work in our day-to-day lives every week.

Sometimes the stories are of apparent failure. Our friends Anna and Sam invited all their neighbours round for food. None of them came! We all cheered them anyway, because it is the courage to reach out that counts, not the result. In the end, their actions led to neighbours getting in touch and new friendships being formed. Often the stories are just about small things where people have noticed God in their everyday life, or have offered to pray for someone, or did an act of kindness. But what happens is that if I don't have a story, it makes me wonder why, and pushes me back to prayer and to action. Often we have found that the storytelling section goes on for so long that I have to make my talk shorter as a result!

All of the stories are tiny glimpses of New Creation. They are rivers in the desert and streams in the wilderness. They are signposts to something greater. They weave together in the making of all things new. They are tasters of the fruit of the Promised Land. They paint a picture of the gospel.

Here are some of the glimpses of the New Creation we have seen in Langworthy recently.

During the pandemic lockdowns, our team at our LifeCentre community hub visited up to seventy families a week, providing pastoral support, food and prayer. On one occasion as Liz prayed for someone on their doorstep, they said that it felt like church! This was a little glimpse of the New Creation. Others have been helping with the vaccination programme here in Salford, providing hope for thousands of people trapped for months in the many lockdowns.

The NHS workers, education and shop workers in our church have been courageously serving alongside their colleagues during this whole time. My brother Andrew and his wife, Natalie, have been visiting the kids in our church to keep them focused on Jesus at a time when it has been impossible to gather in person, as well as producing countless videos telling the Christian story for primary school kids. Before the lockdowns they were heavily involved in Christian RE provision in the local schools, including two prayer weeks every year which meant that 1,000 local children got to spend an hour each in a prayer room, tasting the beauty of the presence of God. They also have a Christian group in each school for any children who wish to explore the Christian faith further, which are regularly attended by twenty-five to thirty kids in each session. People have been reaching out to their neighbours like never before, offering prayer and practical support.

Beth, who manages our LifeCentre, has been heavily involved in working to address the issues of holiday hunger in Salford. Her incredible work has led to the council being on the cutting edge of holiday provision for those in need, and she has helped to spearhead the delivery of provision this summer for up to 2,500 children across the city. Every child who receives nutritional food and a fun, welcoming place to be this summer, where they would have had none, is getting a glimpse of the New Creation where no child will go hungry and no person will be alone.

Our friend Rachel, who has been providing fitness classes and running groups that improve well-being and create community among local women, and Dave, who runs a flag football team for local people, are providing glimpses of the New Creation when there will be no more sickness and pain, and loneliness will be a thing of the past (Revelation 21:4). My wife, Esther, heads up our breakfast group for local children with difficult home situations, providing a family atmosphere around the breakfast table and improving their attendance, attainment and behaviour at school. This too is a signpost of the coming kingdom of God, where all are welcome at the table, and the lonely are put in families (Psalm 68:6).

A local solicitor gives her time to offer her skills, offering free advice on family law. We have musicians writing and singing songs that tell our stories and lead us into encounters with God. My son, Daniel, my daughter, Rebekah, and my nieces play instruments in our worship for church, offering their skills in worship to Jesus. All these things point us towards what is to come when Jesus makes 'everything new'.

The other churches I have mentioned in this book – in Stenhouse, Barton, Bolton and The Groves – each of them could tell many more stories of their own signs of the kingdom, their own foretastes of the New Creation. Each of them could explain how, in small and imperfect ways, their congregations are hermeneutics of the gospel. Each of us resonates with Paul's comments in 1 Thessalonians 2:8: 'Because we loved you so much, we were delighted to share with you not only the gospel of God but our whole lives as well.'

When God gives you His heart for a people and a place, it is a delight to share the gospel and your life with them. It is a privilege to be with the Lord who is 'close to the broken-hearted, and saves those crushed in spirit' (Psalm 34:18), and to share in that brokenness and experience healing for yourself.

Conclusion

What am I hoping you have gained from reading this book? I hope that if you are in a difficult situation in your life, or if you are working in a tough area and seeing little apparent fruit, that you have been encouraged to keep going. Don't give up. I hope that in the stories I have told and in the Big Story that has framed the book, you will have found hope and some inspiration. I hope the stories have been 'verbal acts of hospitality',[32] and that you have felt welcome in these pages. I hope you have nodded your head and breathed a few sighs of relief as you have remembered you're not the only one who struggles. I hope my attempts to be honest will enable you to be honest with yourself and others.

I would love to hear your stories and see what I can learn from you and your community. I would love to hear the songs of your community, and what the gospel sounds like in your place and to your people. I would be really interested to see in what ways the things you say and do give others a glimpse of the gospel of Jesus.

I would be thrilled if some of you who started this book feeling like giving up and being convinced that you are a failure, will now realise that you are not a failure and will

---

[32] Peterson, *Christ Plays in Ten Thousand Places*, p13.

receive the courage you need to carry on with what God has called you to do. Or perhaps, just as courageously, you will find the motivation to bring an end to a plant or project, if that is what you know God is calling you to do. Often we need to go through such deaths before we see resurrection.

For others, I hope that you decide to go to the toughest places you can find and plant yourself there and see what happens when you live out the gospel as people of the New Creation. I hope some of you quit the well-paid jobs you are doing, trust God to provide for you and find Jesus reigniting your soul as you embrace the messiness and vulnerability of the upside down kingdom of God (if Jesus tells you to). I pray that you will gain a fresh confidence in the utter trustworthiness of Jesus Christ. I hope that you are freed from addictions, from fear of death and from the need to please people. I hope that some of you realise that your job is part of the New Creation project and not just something you do to earn money. I pray that you will fall more in love with Jesus, remembering that nothing is better than Him. Today I would love it if you decide to start reading the Bible all the way through every year for the rest of your life, each year finding yourself again in the story of God.

What are your hopes? What do you take away from these stories? Where did you find yourself in the Big Story? Since I wrote my first book four years ago we have had the very hardest times as a church since we started pursuing this whole calling in the late 1990s. But I have known God in a deeper way than ever, and experienced His presence more intensely and profoundly than before. I am still praying for revival as we did at the start, but now it doesn't look like stadiums full of bouncing worshippers. It looks like tables of welcome and healing and transformation. It looks like flowers pushing through cracks in the pavement and providing vulnerable beauty. It looks like the kingfisher that we have seen near a dirty stream in Salford, flying past a discarded trolley and providing a glimpse of another world. It sounds like the laughter of my friends who have sustained and challenged me, and the joy last week when we felt the tangible presence of God when we sang songs to Jesus outside the school. It is the story of Joe who discovered that he was not forgotten. It is my fire pit with friends gathered round, toasting marshmallows, sharing our lives and praying together. It is the remarkable perseverance of people mentioned in this book who are planting churches in places seen as spiritual deserts, but who are discovering streams and springs and people of peace.

May you have courage today to obey Jesus. May you be inspired to love Him more. May you meet Him in the bread and wine, in the faces of those in need, in the tears of your children (if you have them). May He be revealed to you as you wash dishes, squirt hand sanitiser, forgive someone who has hurt you, pray for someone for healing. May you remember that nothing is better than Jesus.

Arise, shine, for your light has come,
and the glory of the LORD rises upon you.
See, darkness covers the earth
and thick darkness is over the peoples,
but the LORD rises upon you
and his glory appears over you.
Nations will come to your light,
and kings to the brightness of your dawn.

Lift up your eyes and look about you:
All assemble and come to you;
your sons come from afar,
and your daughters are carried on the hip.
Then you will look and be radiant,
your heart will throb and swell with joy;
the wealth on the seas will be brought to you,
to you the riches of the nations will come. ...

Although you have been forsaken and hated,
with no one travelling through,
I will make you the everlasting pride
and the joy of all generations.
You will drink the milk of nations
and be nursed at royal breasts.
Then you will know that I, the LORD, am your
Saviour,
your Redeemer, the Mighty One of Jacob.
Instead of bronze I will bring you gold,
and silver in place of iron.
Instead of wood I will bring you bronze,
and iron in place of stones.
I will make peace your governor
and well-being your ruler.

No longer will violence be heard in your land,
nor ruin or destruction within your borders,
but you will call your walls Salvation
and your gates Praise.
The sun will no more be your light by day,
nor will the brightness of the moon shine on you,
for the LORD will be your everlasting light,
and your God will be your glory.
Your sun will never set again,
and your moon will wane no more;
the LORD will be your everlasting light,
and your days of sorrow will end.
Then all your people will be righteous
and they will possess the land for ever.
They are the shoot I have planted,
the work of my hands,
for the display of my splendour.
The least of you will become a thousand,
the smallest a mighty nation.
I am the LORD;
in its time I will do this swiftly.
(Isaiah 60:1-5, 15-22)